PRAISE FOR *CHANGING LAWS, SAVING LIVES*

"This book ruined a perfectly good night's sleep, but that was my fault for picking it up after sundown. Little did I suspect that a 'law book' would glue my eyeballs to every page. Suspense, awe, thrills, bad guys galore, and justice at the end. Along the way, a compelling autobiography, and a generous trove of secrets for trial lawyer success, told with panache and New Mexican spice. This book has it all."

—Patrick Malone, co-author of *Rules of the Road*, author of *Winning Medical Malpractice Cases*, member of the Inner Circle of Advocates

"As captivating as a legal thriller and as informative as any textbook, *Changing Laws, Saving Lives* is the rare work that manages to mix concrete guidance with encompassing insights—leaving the reader entertained, informed, and inspired. It is a must-read for trial lawyers, law students who aspire to join their ranks, and all those who care about the on-the-ground operation of the American civil justice system."

—Nora Freeman Engstrom, Professor of Law, Stanford Law School

"This book will engage and inform you, whatever your level of experience. It is a rich, informative, and compelling story told by a master storyteller. No wonder her verdicts are legendary!"

—Roxane Barton Conlin, first woman president of the American Association for Justice, member of the Inner Circle of Advocates

"This book reads like a novel while exposing trial techniques, tactics, and strategies. [It's] better than a half-day CLE, and faster."

—Roger Dodd, coauthor of *Cross-Examination Skills for Law Students*, listed in *Superlawyers* for both Florida and Georgia

"Superb trial strategies delivered in a story like a John Grisham thriller. A must-read for the serious trial lawyer."

—Judith Livingston, Lawyer of the Year in 2011 and 2013, *Best Lawyers Magazine*, New York

"Randi writes like she tries a case—with drama, compassion, and surprise endings. Read this book to learn from it and for sheer enjoyment!"

"Full of plain-spoken, heartfelt, and inspiring litigation techniques. Randi provides hundreds of invaluable tips on being a better lawyer, and wraps that advice inside compelling stories that stick with you. Not only is it easy to read, Randi writes as if she is speaking frankly to a jury in a courtroom. You will be swept up by her passion and creativity!"

Roger —

My fellow courtroom warrior. Thank you for helping with this, my first book. You are the best!

Randi

12/8/14

CHANGING LAWS, SAVING LIVES

How to Take On Corporate Giants and Win

RANDI McGINN

TRIAL GUIDES, LLC

Trial Guides, LLC, Portland, Oregon 97210

Copyright © 2014 by Randi McGinn. All rights reserved.

TRIAL GUIDES and logo are registered trademarks of Trial Guides, LLC.

ISBN: 978-1-941007-20-4

Library of Congress Control Number: 2014950996

Trial Guides, LLC
Attn: Permissions
2350 NW York Street
Portland, OR 97210
(800) 309-6845
www.trialguides.com

Interior design by Laura Lind Design and Erin E. Davis

Jacket design by Chris Tegethoff

The photographs appearing on pages 11, 12, 53, 66, 89, 97, 98, 140, 150, 187, 188, and 206 are used with the kind permission of the people depicted in each photograph or their families. The photographs appearing on pages 81, 82, 118, and 122 are screen captures of depositions that were videotaped in connection with the cases discussed in this book. The photographs appearing on page 20 are screen captures from security camera footage that was produced in discovery. The photographs on pages 22, 26, 92, and 208 are photographs that the author's law firm partners or staff took in conjunction with the relevant cases. The photograph on page 49 and the author's photo on the back cover are by Kip Malone. The illustrations and diagrams on pages 26 and 51 were created by the author or her law firm in conjunction with the relevant cases. All photographs are used for purposes of criticism, comment, news reporting, teaching, scholarship, and research under the Fair Use Doctrine.

Printed and bound in the United States of America.

This book is printed on acid-free paper.

10 9 8 7 6 5 4 3 2 1

ALSO BY RANDI MCGINN

Creating Magic in Trial (CD/DVD)

In the last short story published before his death, Mark Twain imagined heaven as a place where a cobbler who had the soul of a poet wouldn't have to make shoes and where a procession of the greatest people in the world included not just Shakespeare and Buddha and Homer, but a line of unknown people whose greatness had never been recognized on earth because they had to work to take care of their families.[1]

I imagine there were many unknown, unsung women in that celestial line—women who, because of the century or country into which they were born, were never allowed to use their prodigious intellect, business acumen, or political savvy to help their communities. This book is for them.

---

1. Mark Twain, "Captain Stormfield's Visit to Heaven," *Harper's Magazine*, December, 1907 and January, 1908.

Contents

Publisher's Note

This book is intended for practicing attorneys. This book does not offer legal advice and does not take the place of consultation with an attorney or other professional with appropriate expertise and experience.

Attorneys are strongly cautioned to evaluate the information, ideas, and opinions set forth in this book in light of their own research, experience, and judgment; to consult applicable rules, regulations, procedures, cases, and statutes (including those issued after the publication date of this book); and to make independent decisions about whether and how to apply such information, ideas, and opinions to a particular case.

Quotations from cases, pleadings, discovery, and other sources are for illustrative purposes only and may not be suitable for use in litigation in any particular case.

The cases described in this book are real cases. Sometimes the details are taken from transcripts, pleadings, and other court documents, and sometimes they are based on the author's trial notes and recollections.

All references to the trademarks of third parties are strictly informational and for purposes of commentary. No sponsorship or endorsement by, or affiliation with, the trademark owners is claimed or implied by the author or publisher of this book.

The author and publisher disclaim any liability or responsibility for loss or damage resulting from the use of this book or the information, ideas, or opinions contained in this book.

FOREWORD

Since I graduated in 1966, I have tried hundreds of civil and criminal cases over a career spanning nearly fifty years. I have met many brilliant trial lawyers over those years, but none more brilliant than the author of this book, Randi McGinn. On every page of this book, there are suggestions and insights which will be useful to not only the new lawyer, but also the seasoned lawyer.

Of particular value is Randi's handling of problems unique to women trial lawyers. What do you wear? What do you say? How do you react to sexism? Do women bring something special to the table? How do we make use of whatever we can bring?

One of the failures of many books by lawyers is the total lack of photos. Apparently, attorney-authors who generally understand the rules of persuasion do not apply those rules when writing for other lawyers. Randi shows us what the murdered mother looked like, how her children and her mother looked, how the convenience store was configured, and many other things that enrich our experience and help us to understand and visualize what happened to this young woman. The addition of relevant photos enhances not only our understanding of the story but also of the losses this family suffered.

Transformative law is another unusual and important topic Randi covers. Like Randi's clients, mine are not particularly interested in money. Most of them want to hold the wrongdoer accountable so that, in so far as possible, whatever happened to them or their loved one does not happen to anyone else. It is inevitably the one thing every single client mentions every single time in our first meeting. Like Randi, we often include as a part of settlement some positive action that will help to protect others.

In the first third-party criminal case I ever filed, my client was a good friend who was raped in her own apartment, in her own bed, by an assailant who came through a sliding window which would not lock and about which she had complained in writing three times and orally many more. In Iowa, we could have filed the case anonymously, but instead, we called a press conference, and in her own name and her own voice, she called for increased safety for single women living in apartments.

In a case involving the sexual molestation of four young children, we found that the molester, who was on the sexual offender list, was hired as a maintenance man at a low-income family apartment complex. The management had actual notice that he had been convicted of sexual assault on two children under the age of thirteen. As part of our settlement with the landlord, we insisted that the agreement include a requirement that every employee, full- and part-time, have a complete criminal background check.

In employment discrimination cases, it is common to require an apology. In bullying cases, transformative law may include a training program, an independent investigation, and written document of the findings.

This book will engage and inform you, whatever your level of experience. It is a rich, informative, and compelling story told by a master storyteller. No wonder her verdicts are legendary!

—Roxane Barton Conlin

ACKNOWLEDGMENTS

Any lawyer stands upon the shoulders of others who are generous enough to share what they have learned in the courtroom. All I am, I owe to others—my professors at UNM Law School, my brothers and sisters in the Inner Circle, my friends at NITA, NCDC and AAJ's NCA, my creative and talented law partners and staff, and my true love and sounding board, Charles Daniels. And then there are my children, who taught me the lesson of unconditional love.

This book would not have happened without the encouragement of Rick Friedman, the faith of publisher Aaron DeShaw and the enthusiastic support of editor Tina Ricks.

Downloadable Content

This book references a number of items such as affidavits, documents, PowerPoint slides, video clips, and other items that you can download and read or watch. These files give you concrete examples of Randi McGinn's methods and techniques.

To download these files to your computer, smartphone, or tablet, go to the following link:

http://www.trialguides.com/resources/downloads/changing-laws

INTRODUCTION

It was the biggest case our all-woman law firm had ever handled.

Our clients were the three surviving children of Elizabeth Garcia. She was a twenty-six-year-old woman who, on the second night of her new job working alone on the graveyard shift in an Allsup's convenience store, was robbed, kidnapped, raped, stabbed fifty-six times, and left for dead in a dark, lonely field in Hobbs, New Mexico.[1]

For six long years since her death, the five New Mexico attorneys on the other side of the case had done everything in their power to prevent us from getting the evidence we needed, and tried to make sure a jury never heard the case. After finding witnesses, gathering the evidence on our own, responding to—and arguing— a mountain of written motions in court, we were just ten days away from trial. Ready, we thought, to finally hold this convenience store chain accountable for years of forcing its minimum-wage clerks to work alone at night without any security.

Then came the e-mail from a friend, Paul Luvera, a marvelous trial attorney from Seattle, Washington, who had recently tried a case defended by the same insurance company, AIG, one of the largest in the country. His e-mail went something like this:

---

1. *Mary Ann McConnell, as personal representative of the Estate of Elizabeth Garcia, deceased, and as next friend of Xavier Mendoza, Jerome Mendoza, and Cene Mendoza, minor children*, First Judicial District Court, County of Santa Fe, New Mexico, case number D-0101-CV-200500045.

I hear you are about to try a case against a corporation insured by AIG insurance. I thought you might like to know what you can expect. Without warning, a week before trial, they will bring in a team of attorneys from a large Atlanta, Georgia, law firm to take over the defense alongside your local lawyers. Backing up the five to six lawyers in the courtroom [there would be nine in our case], there will be an army of other attorneys back at the office cranking out written motions every night to distract you from your trial preparation.

The Friday before trial, they will, for the first time, let you know they are bringing in a shadow jury [something I had never heard of until this e-mail]. Hired by a jury consultant and paid $150 to $250 a day [far more than the fourteen real jurors were paid], the shadow jury will sit in the back of the courtroom and, without ever knowing which side hired them, will report their impressions every night to the other side so they can adjust their witnesses and their defenses while the trial is going on.[2]

How did I feel when this e-mail arrived? You know the scene from the 2007 movie *300*, where King Leonidas and his three hundred Spartan warriors look out from the pass they are defending to get their first glimpse of the Persian horde, an army of more than a million warriors, which they will have to fight in the battle of Thermopylae? It was like that.

How could a small law firm like ours ever get justice for this family when the nation's largest insurance company was willing to throw unlimited financial resources against us? Given those odds, were we really ready for battle? What in the world made me think a girl who graduated from high school in Alamogordo, New Mexico, and attended a state college and law school could ever stand up in a courtroom and be a trial lawyer against people like this?

---

2. Paul Luvera, e-mail message to the author.

And then my friend provided the answer. "Don't worry," he said. "By the end of the case, they will be more afraid of you than you are of them."

It turns out he was right.

1

FINDING A STORY WORTH
TELLING

Being a trial lawyer is the greatest job in the world. This is especially true for women, who have an advantage in the courtroom.[1] Of course, I didn't know that in 1976 when I was trying to find a story worth telling—about my own life and the lives of others.

After getting my undergraduate degree in journalism from New Mexico State University in Las Cruces, I was working as a reporter for the *Ruidoso News*, a biweekly small-town newspaper. In addition to covering local stories, I would write spec articles for national magazines at night and send them off in hopes of breaking into the big time. Instead of national fame, rejection letter after rejection letter came back in the mail. All of it in the same printed format—an indication that the editors hadn't read past the first paragraph, if at all.

My stack of failures drove me to consult the smartest man I knew, my uncle Noel McGinn, a professor at Harvard.

"Why won't anyone read my articles?" I asked him.

---

1. See chapter 21, "You Don't Know a Woman until You've Met Her in Court."

"Why should they?" he said.

Taken aback by his question, I said, "Well, these are good stories I'm writing, plus I'm reasonably bright, insightful, and maybe even a little funny."

"How would they know that?" he asked. "To them, you're just some kid from a place they've never heard of in a state they're not even sure is part of the United States. Now, I know it's probably not fair, but if you had some kind of advanced degree, they might think what you had to say was worth reading. At least it might get you in the door and cause them to read your article."

That's right, I did not go to law school because, like an Olympics gymnast, I knew from the age of three what I wanted to be. I did not start law school with the noble heart of a social crusader who wanted to change the world. I did not even go to law school because it might provide a respectable career path that would make my parents proud. I committed myself to three years of grueling graduate school for the ridiculously suspect reason that a law degree might make people read the stories I wanted to write.

For those of you who are adrift and not sure yet what you want to do in life, the good news is sometimes, by continuing to stumble forward, you find the thing you were always meant to do.

PEOPLE LOVE STORIES

Telling stories is the thing I was meant to do. As the oldest of five children, with just seven years between the first of us and the last, some of my early memories are of storytelling. One summer night when visiting our cousins, we were allowed to run unsupervised through the neighborhood after dark while our parents sipped cocktails. Drunk on the exhilaration of freedom in the warm night air, when we were finally called into the house, none of us could settle down. As the oldest, I was told to keep the kids quiet in a back bedroom while the adults played cards. Outnumbered, I could not wrestle them all into submission. The only thing that worked was telling them a story.

On this night there were no books to read from, so I made up a tale of terror. A tale of boys and girls like those in the bedroom, wandering through dark woods and perilous caves, faced with moral choices between good and evil, and facing terrible consequences when they chose the wrong path. As the story went on, my brother, sisters, and cousins grew quieter and quieter. The younger ones cowered under the covers during the really scary parts of the story, but when I asked if I should stop, their small muffled voices, often tinged with a thrill of fear, would call out, "No, go on, go on!"

Human beings, young and old, love a good story.

LAW IS STORYTELLING

In turns out that being a trial lawyer is storytelling on steroids. As a trial lawyer, not only do I write the script for my opening and closing, but I get to direct the production and play one of the starring roles. If I tell my client's story truly and well, through a miraculous kind of verbal alchemy, I can convince a jury of real people to turn that story into justice.

When you first start out in the practice of law, particularly if you hang up your own shingle, you are just grateful for any case or anyone who walks in the door and trusts you with her legal problem. Once you are past the stage of being able to pay your rent, a successful law practice is built by recognizing the clients who have stories worth telling, who have suffered a wrong worth righting, who have a case that will make a difference not just for one person, but for the community as a whole. These are stories, like the one I told in that bedroom long ago, where those listening (the jurors) can see themselves in the client's predicament and will care about fixing the problem so it will not happen to them.

The problem in selecting a good story to tell, or a good case to take, is that when you are representing the person bringing the lawsuit, you have the burden of proof on the three main legal issues and a fourth unnamed "X" factor not found in any jury instruction:

The Four Factors of a Case

Liability	Did the defendant do something wrong?
Causation	Did the wrong cause the injuries claimed?
Damages	How much will make the person whole?
The "X" Factor	Does this person deserve the money?

If you lose on any one of these issues, you lose the case. The defendant has to prove absolutely nothing. To make the life of a trial lawyer even tougher, if you win all these elements at trial, you may still lose the case through an appeal, which can last an average of two to five years after the verdict. I never said the greatest job in the world didn't come with a few challenges. All the more reason to try and increase your potential client's chances of success by evaluating the case carefully, balancing the four issues you have to prove, and selecting or rejecting the case.

FIND A STORY WORTH TELLING

Connecticut lawyer Mike Koskoff passed on to me the advice of his father, the legendary trial lawyer Ted Koskoff: "You make more money from the cases you turn down than the cases that you take."

So how do you follow that sage counsel and recognize the cases you should take and the cases you should turn down? How do you find out if the person who phones or walks in your front door has a story worth telling?

There are a few basic elements to every story worth telling:

◆ A violation of safety rules involving a danger to the community.

◆ A villain or villains.

◆ A hero or heroine.

◆ A solution from the jury that makes us all safer.

These elements, and how to recognize and develop them, are what this book is all about.

2

A Grandmother's Anguished Question

Elizabeth Garcia

At twenty-six, with her long black hair and 150-watt smile, Elizabeth Garcia was a woman on the road to a better life. She had been sidetracked for a while in a bad relationship with a man who left her alone to raise their three children, Xavier (called "X"), age seven, Jerome, age five, and Cene (pronounced

Sin-nay), age four. For Christmas 2001, the children's absent father had promised to send Elizabeth $600 to buy presents. She was counting on that money, but it didn't come through.

Rather than disappoint her children, she swallowed her pride and asked her mom for help to buy a tree for the house and a few presents. It wasn't grand, but it was enough. Elizabeth made up her mind that she would never rely on someone else to take care of her kids again. She would figure out how to move ahead and support them all in her small town of Hobbs, New Mexico.

As soon as the holidays were over, Liz quit her day job as a clerk at the AutoZone auto parts store, and enrolled in the local community college with the goal of becoming a teacher. She would go to school by day and, once the kids were asleep, would work for minimum wage on the graveyard shift in the Southwest's largest convenience store chain, Allsup's. While her brother watched her sleeping kids, she could study for the next day's class on what she assumed would be a low-volume sales shift. Elizabeth Garcia was a salt-of-the-earth unsung heroine, a single working mother holding up the world on her back for the betterment of her family.

Jerome, Cene, and Xavier, Christmas 2001

After two days spent following another clerk around on the day shift in a store in town, Allsup's assigned this female Atlas to work in the store farthest from Hobbs, in an isolated location on the Lovington Highway. Stocked with beer and hard liquor, the store had no security—no video cameras, no high-intensity lighting, and no secure location where a clerk could retreat from danger. On top of all that, Allsup's required her to work alone on the graveyard shift.

Elizabeth's first night on the graveyard shift at the Lovington Highway Allsup's Store No. 146, some men came in and robbed her of a case a beer. Concerned, she asked a friend to stop by the next night, her second night of work, January 15, 2002. At approximately 2:30 a.m. the next morning, the friend stopped at the store and found it empty. He called Liz's brother, who got someone to stay with the kids and rushed to the store. There, on the counter, was Liz's open algebra book from the community college classes she had started that week. Her brother called her name and frantically searched the store, but Elizabeth had vanished. Her backpack, purse, coat, and car were all still there. The cash register was empty. The last record on the cash register was at 2:24 a.m.—a "no sale" to open the drawer so the robber could get at the money.

Elizabeth had followed the one rule that Allsup's instructed her to follow: keep low amounts of cash in the register. Allsup's management quickly determined that only $12 had been stolen. Perhaps angered by the small amount of money, the robber had taken the only thing of real value in the store: Elizabeth Garcia. With Elizabeth still missing and a search underway by the police, the Allsup's convenience store was back up and running before dawn with another lone worker called out to staff the counter.

Elizabeth's family, her brother, mother, younger sister, and extended family gathered at her house in Hobbs with her children to wait for word. Later that afternoon, a police car pulled up to the house with a chaplain in the passenger seat. The police officer walked into the living room and was immediately surrounded by family. He looked into their upturned faces and dashed the last rays of hope he saw in their eyes.

"They found Elizabeth in a field a few miles away from the store," he said. "She had been raped, stabbed fifty-six times, and had her throat cut."

In the rush to hear what they hoped was good news, no one noticed that seven-year-old Xavier was also standing in the room. Upon hearing that his mother was dead, he ran out into the front yard and began to scream.

So who was the villain in this case? Certainly, the unknown man who kidnapped Elizabeth and murdered her in a lonely field was as despicable a villain as could be imagined. Because there were no video cameras to capture the kidnapping, the killer would not be found for another two years, after he raped and killed a second woman and police matched his DNA to Elizabeth Garcia's case.

But was this criminal the whole story? Did the convenience store bear some blame for requiring a woman to work alone on the graveyard shift without any security? Were nighttime convenience stores so dangerous that requiring a woman to work alone at night was akin to the scene from the movie *Jurassic Park*, where a goat is staked out alone to attract the predatory Tyrannosaurus Rex? Or was this convenience store chain an innocent business like any other that simply provided jobs, gas, and late-night snacks for the community?

Our first inkling of the true nature of the Allsup's convenience store chain came in the initial call to our office from Victorina Garcia, Elizabeth's mother and the children's grandmother. It was upon Victorina, the Director of the District Office of the Department of Labor, who worked in nearby Roswell, New Mexico, that the burden of Elizabeth's death fell the heaviest. It was Victorina who would take the three children into her small house, where they had to subdivide the family room with a sheet to make enough bedrooms for the kids.

It was upon Victorina that fell the task of burying her daughter. She arranged the funeral and paid for it out of her meager savings, savings she would now need to raise Elizabeth's three children. When she submitted the $7,000 funeral bill to Allsup's to be paid for by workers' compensation insurance, the company rejected the payment. The reason? Because Elizabeth was taken from the store, it was their position that she had not been killed on the job. The adjuster even implied that Elizabeth might have left her post voluntarily to go off with some man.

Victorina knew her daughter was a responsible and dependable person. Just as she had not abandoned her children, she would never abandon her post at a job to go off with a man. She was offended by Allsup's accusation and knew that what the company was doing was wrong. She picked up the phone and called our all-woman law firm in Albuquerque.

The great irony was that, had Allsup's just done the right thing and paid for Elizabeth's funeral, like many people who have suffered a great loss and are drowning in their grief, Victorina Garcia would likely never have contacted a lawyer.

Victorina asked one simple, anguished question: "Wasn't there something we could do to get justice for Elizabeth?"

The answer was not so simple. Two legal problems stood in the way of finding justice for Elizabeth.

First, the only way a lawsuit could be filed against Elizabeth's employer outside of the Workers' Compensation Act (which allowed recovery of two-thirds of her minimum wage, paid out only until her children reached eighteen) was if we could find evidence that Allsup's knew Elizabeth's working conditions were dangerous. We had to prove that they decided to make Elizabeth work alone without security, recklessly and intentionally, with knowledge that it placed Elizabeth at risk of death or great bodily harm. Negligent conduct alone would not be enough to hold Allsup's accountable.

Like nearly all of our clients, Victorina Garcia did not have the money to pay lawyers on an hourly basis to investigate this case against a company with unlimited funds to defend itself. Our fee would be on a contingency basis. If we were able to reach a settlement or collect on a verdict, we would be paid one-third of the recovery. If we took the case and couldn't find enough evidence to make the heavy lift of proving the convenience store chain's reckless decision-making, we would receive nothing for all the work and investigation put into the case.

Second, the jury would be allowed to compare the intentional acts of the killer with the reckless acts of the employer and assign percentages of fault. If the killer was found 95 percent responsible and the company 5 percent at fault, the company would owe the family only 5 percent of any damages. If the killer was found 100 percent at fault, the family would recover nothing.

We told Victorina Garcia about these two significant legal hurdles. We told her that because of these unknowns, we could not promise her we would ultimately be successful, and the case might be dismissed on legal grounds before trial. We told her that even if we could get over these hurdles, we might not have our day in court for years. Even then, we could lose if we had a bad jury, lose if the jury found negligence but not recklessness, lose if the jury did not find causation, or lose if the jury placed all the blame on the killer. Even if we won at trial, we told her she could lose on appeal.

We told her all of the bad things that could happen so she could make a knowledgeable and clear-eyed decision about the hard path that is litigation. After learning all of this, her courage did not flag for a moment. She told us to go ahead and find out what had happened.

3

Standing in Your Client's Shoes

Visiting the Scene

The best place to begin an investigation is the place where your client was harmed. There are things you come to understand only by driving on the same highway where a semitruck crossed the median, by clambering up onto the same Kress coal hauler (a huge truck used in smelting ore) upon which your client was burned to death, or by standing behind the same lonely convenience store counter where a woman was kidnapped.

When I graduated from law school, I never imagined that my law degree would take me, and my team of lawyers, to any of the following locations:

- We went to an underground uranium mine, deep in the bowels of the earth, to learn how a man was crushed to death by an unsecured rock ceiling that dropped tons of rock on his head.

- We investigated a factory floor in Georgia, to learn how cuts in maintenance of the steamer vats resulted in the first outbreak of botulism in commercially canned foods in twenty years.

- We visited the boardroom of a national hospital corporation, to learn how cost cutting, through understaffing and the increased use of nurses rather than doctors, resulted in an anoxic brain injury to a young man who came to the emergency room for help when he started having problems with his breathing.

VISIT THE SCENE FOR EVERY CASE

If you are blessed with the gift of intellectual curiosity, being a trial lawyer is never boring. Every case that walks in the door starts with learning something new. After learning your client's story, you must go out to visit the scene and stand in your client's shoes. You cannot fully understand a case from the antiseptic confines of your office. No video, picture, or diagram can replace an actual visit to the place where the events occurred. You have to go out and experience the place yourself and not through the eyes of your investigator; if that means a road trip, so much the better for office bonding.

From a simple visit to the scene in past cases I have discovered the following:

- An eight-foot adobe wall that stood between the place where a police officer was standing and the location where he said he saw my client do something illegal.

- In the totaled truck of the drunk driver who killed two couples from Nebraska, we found paperwork showing his BIA (Bureau of Indian Affairs) supervisors knew about his past arrests for drunk driving, but let him have a government vehicle anyway.

- The Norman Rockwellian, tree-lined, upper-middle-class neighborhood, where a young man stood in his backyard in his pajamas, playing with his dog one sunny morning. This was the last place anyone would expect two men in jeans to break down the fence and shoot him in the back three times. We also never expected that the two men in plainclothes turned out to be police officers serving a two-month-old traffic warrant, which only made the shooting in this idyllic setting even more horrific.

VISITING A HOSPITAL

In one case, my law partner Elicia Montoya visited the hospital where twenty-six-year-old Joseph Mendoza was left to languish in the waiting room.[1] She discovered video cameras in the waiting room and throughout the hospital. The cameras in the waiting room confirmed that Joseph's mother had gone to the desk three different times to get help for her son, who was having difficulty breathing as a result of the onset of epiglottitis.

Most importantly, there was a video camera outside the X-ray room where, after his mother insisted her son be treated or tested, the technician violated the rules for suspected epiglottitis and left Joseph alone in the room. It was in that room where his throat finally closed completely and he was deprived of oxygen, drowning on dry land.

A request for all the video footage of Joseph—the video footage we only knew about because of Elicia's visit to the hospital—was one of the things that ultimately helped resolve the case.

On the same day of the malpractice, the hospital risk manager recognized that this brain injury should not have happened and litigation might follow. Within a few days she had pulled all of the digital video footage of Joseph, with which she created her own timeline of the events. Then, mysteriously, all of the video footage was preserved—except the shots from the video camera

---

1. *Susan Weckesser, as Conservator of the Estate of Joseph Mendoza, an adult incapacitated person, Hector Mendoza and Stella Mendoza v. PHC-Las Cruces*, First Judicial District Court, case number D-101-CV-2010-00452.

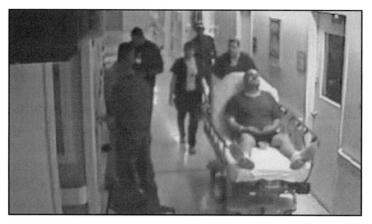

Joseph Mendoza going into the X-ray suite

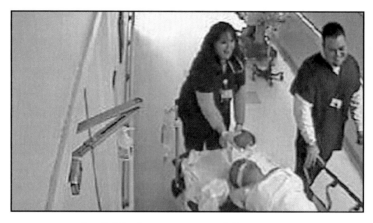

Joseph Mendoza coming out of the X-ray suite

immediately outside the X-ray room where Joseph lost his airway and was permanently brain-damaged.

What would the missing video have shown? It would have helped us confirm how long he had been without oxygen (perhaps as long as thirteen to fifteen minutes) when hospital staff first discovered him, how long it took for them to bring the wrong crash cart, realize they had the wrong one, and then call for another. It would have revealed the medical staff's faces as they were summoned to the room to deal with the blockage of this young man's airway and whether they were in a state of panic, fear, or something even worse: complacence.

Luckily the cameras up the hallway showed him being wheeled into the X-ray suite, his head back, trying to keep his airway open so he could breathe.

Another camera showed the aftermath of the hospital's terrible series of mistakes—the now brain-injured Joseph being wheeled out, about to become the youngest person in a nursing home full of old people. He was unable to walk, feed himself, or ever speak a word to his family again.

A cover-up like the erasing of the key videotape footage makes even the most innocuous actions look nefarious. The hospital resolved the case rather than explain to a jury what happened to the lost videotape and worse, what happened to our client.

VISITING A THREE-WAY STOP

In another case, we visited the three-way stop where twenty-two-year-old Jason Wachocki (pronounced Va-hut-ski) was T-boned and killed by a corrections officer on his way to work at the Bernalillo County Metropolitan Detention Center.[2] That visit gave us an idea about how to prove our case. As we walked the intersection with our accident reconstruction expert, we watched car after car, including police cars, blow through the same intersection at high speeds on their way to the jail. What was going on?

We had stumbled upon an eight-mile stretch of two-lane highway that our local sheriff's office had tacitly declared a lawless zone, where no one enforced or obeyed traffic laws. The reason? Over the objections of law enforcement and the corrections department, the county had moved the jail from its convenient location downtown to an isolated spot seventeen miles west of the city. This meant that, if they wanted to arrest someone, police officers had to throw the

---

2. *Michael and Tia Wachocki v. The City of Albuquerque*, Second Judicial District Court, State of New Mexico, Bernalillo County, case number CV-2005 07788.

arrestee in the back of the patrol car, drive seventeen miles out of town, book them, and then return to their beat, a process that took two to three hours.

In protest, once they got off the freeway onto the two-lane frontage road, law enforcement and corrections officers sped up far beyond the 40 mph speed limit, illegally passing slower vehicles and running the two sets of stop signs on this roadway. When traveling the road at nighttime (because the jail was open 24-7), officers took to turning off their headlights as they approached the stop signs to see if there were any headlights coming in the opposite direction. If they saw none, they did not slow down and ran the stop sign.

Despite two years of complaints from the two other businesses out in this isolated spot—an auto-racing track and the city waste management department—the sheriff's office did not obey or enforce the traffic laws on the eight-mile stretch of roadway.

The corrections officer who hit our client was aware of this practice. On the night of the collision, he turned off his headlights as he sped toward the three-way stop. Jason, a racetrack safety worker, was coming home after the races were over. He stopped, looked to his left, and, seeing nothing, pulled into the intersection.

The intersection where Jason Wachocki died

The corrections officer broadsided his car at approximately 80 mph, knocking his vehicle sideways, 200 feet down the roadway, and killing him instantly.

An Idea from the Scene

As we stood in the spot where Jason died, we had an idea about how to prove this dangerous, illegal practice. On the edge of the racetrack property, right near the place where Jason stopped at the stop sign, there was a light pole. With the track's permission, we attached a video camera to the pole and recorded ninety-two days of activity at the three-way stop sign.

Night and day, police cruisers, corrections buses, and vans ran that stop sign, singly and in caravans of police vehicles, in sight of each other. It was difficult to find anybody who followed the traffic laws and stopped at the stop sign. That videotape, which our visit to the scene inspired, was worth more than a thousand words, and it was the key to winning the case.[3]

Start your case by going to the scene and standing in your client's shoes. You will discover things you never imagined.

What would we discover in Hobbs, New Mexico, where Elizabeth Garcia was trying to make a new life for her family by working late night in an Allsup's convenience store?

---

3. Clips of this video, called "Video Jason Wachocki," are available at http://www.trialguides.com/resources/downloads/changing-laws.

4

ELIZABETH GARCIA'S LAST WORKPLACE

As you drive into Hobbs, New Mexico, your nose begins to crinkle at the scent of something pungent in the air. Some say it is the smell of money, others claim it is the odor of down-home American enterprise. You can spot the source on the outskirts of town—bobbing metal ponies pumping the oil and gas that are the lifeblood of this desert town.

Without college, the men in Hobbs can make $50,000 a year or more, risking their fingers, backs, and sometimes their lives in the oilfields. Without any higher education, the women in Hobbs are mostly consigned to waitressing or other minimum-wage jobs.

With a population of twenty-eight thousand to forty-three thousand people that fluctuates with the boom and bust of the oil industry, Hobbs was big enough to support two competing convenience store chains. There were six Town and Country stores and ten Allsup's stores. Nine of the Allsup's stores were within city limits. The tenth store was on the edge of town in an isolated location out on the Lovington Highway. It was a place where, at night, there was no one around to hear you scream.

Map of Allsup's stores in Hobbs, New Mexico

The Allsup's store on the Lovington Highway where Elizabeth was kidnapped

The Lovington Highway store was where Elizabeth Garcia was required to work, alone, on the graveyard shift. A cheaply constructed, white cinderblock rectangle, this store was open twenty-four hours a day, seven days a week. The lone clerk was never allowed to close and lock the doors, but had to let anyone and everyone in. The store was stocked with cigarettes, beer, and hard liquor for the men traveling the roadway to and from the oilfields.

After dark, there was no high-intensity perimeter lighting in the parking lot or surrounding area, creating a fishbowl effect that allowed someone in the dark parking lot to observe the inside of the store without being seen. Some of the lights over the gas pumps were burned out, and even the building itself was poorly lit.

The store had no video surveillance cameras anywhere on the premises. There was no "safe room" for the clerk to retreat to and lock herself into if threatened. There was no bullet-resistant enclosure from which a clerk could safely work after hours.

There was a safe place for the money in the store. Installed near the cash register was a drop-safe with impenetrable steel walls, where clerks were required to place all money except for the $50 or less they were to keep in the cash register. If robbed of more than the $50, clerks could be fired. The alarm was in the register. Although it was usually broken, when it worked, the clerk activated it by pulling out particular bills.

Convex mirrors were installed in the corners inside the store so that the clerks could watch for shoplifters. If the lone clerk was too busy to watch the mirrors and prevent shoplifting, she could be fired if there was too much theft—or "shrinkage"—in the store.

My law partners Allegra Carpenter and Elicia Montoya and I visited this Allsup's store several times during the course of the case, but our first visit left the most powerful impression. At this store, the Allsup family had invested in security devices to protect their money and their merchandise, but had spent nothing to protect the lives of the clerks working for them. The clerks were required to act as human shields, risking their own lives for minimum wage to prevent a robber from stealing cash, or a shoplifter from stealing beer and cigarettes.

The Allsup family, who started, owned, and ran this convenience store empire, did not require the same sacrifice of themselves. The corporate offices in Clovis, New Mexico—for CEO father Lonnie Allsup, matriarch Barbara Allsup, and son and acting manager Mark Allsup—were not open after dark and were not easily accessible to the public even during the day. The building had limited access and was equipped with an alarm, a security system, and cameras. During daylight work hours, there was always more than one person on the premises. No one was ever robbed, raped, or murdered on these secure premises.

Our visit to the places where Elizabeth Garcia last worked and died not only revealed the scary conditions under which she spent her last hours, but also provided us a template to begin our investigation into what kinds of security existed to protect convenience store clerks. We discovered that with visits to the stores of the competing Town and Country chain.

Strikingly, while the Allsup's stores had no security, the Town and Country stores had state-of-the-art security cameras, high-intensity lighting on both the perimeter of the parking lot and the building, and two clerks on duty at all times, including on the graveyard shift.

Would these kinds of security measures make a difference in the crime rate or assaults on clerks? We would soon find the answer to that question.

5

Finding a Violation of Safety Rules

After visiting the scene, the next step in preparing your case is to discover the rules that governed the defendant's behavior. The rules the defendant violated, harming not just your client, but making all of us, including the jurors, less safe. Remember: a person will not listen to a story for long if it is not in some way about himself or herself.

Rules and standards are the glue that creates a civilized, safe society. Although we Americans like to stress our spirit of independence, the thing that actually makes us one of the most envied countries in the world is our system of rules and standards that make this country one of the safest places to live on the planet. We are a fascinating contradiction, on one hand voicing our deep distrust of the government and other large institutions, while agreeing for the benefit of the community to follow the rules that our governments, our religions, or our workplaces have established.

RULES ARE OUR SOCIAL COMPACT

The social compact we live by was best described in an essay by Warren Christopher, the former United States secretary of state from 1993 to 1997, in the *This I Believe* series on National Public Radio. Christopher reflects on the trust we place in other drivers, to follow the rules we've all agreed to, so that as a society we can cooperate and thrive:

> I was driving down a two-lane highway at about sixty miles an hour. A car approached from the opposite direction at about the same speed. . . . I was relying on him not to fall asleep, . . . not to cross over into my lane and bring my life suddenly to an end.
>
> At some level, we all depend upon one another. Sometimes that dependence requires us simply to refrain from doing something like crossing over the double yellow line. And sometimes it requires us to act cooperatively, with allies or even with strangers.[1]

Former secretary of state Christopher eloquently captured the way in which—whether loners or gregarious gadabouts—we are all interconnected and depend upon each other to follow the rules in every aspect of modern life.

RULES WE LIVE BY

Every day when you turn on your tap water, you rely on corporations not to have violated the rules about dumping toxic waste, and you rely on the government to test and make sure the water is clean. When you go to a restaurant, you rely on the cooks and owners to follow the health code and you rely on the government

---

1. To read or listen to the rest of this wonderful essay, go to: Warren Christopher, "A Shared Moment of Trust," This I Believe, as heard on NPR's All Things Considered, January 23, 2006, http://thisibelieve.org/essay/6894.

to enforce it, so the food will not make you sick. When you walk down an unlit sidewalk at night, you expect the city or the home-owner will not leave a giant unmarked hole in the walkway. Your neighbors rely on you to do the same with the path to your door.

RULE VIOLATIONS AND THE COMMUNITY

Whether acting negligently, recklessly, or intentionally, people and corporations who do not follow the community's rules, laws, and standards endanger all of us: our friends, our families, and the jurors. A civil lawsuit is the way society holds those people or corporations accountable. If they are not required to pay for the damage they caused by violating the rules or standards, just like undisciplined children, they will continue to violate the rules and risk the lives or health of the rest of us in the community.

Of course, the concept of a violation of the rules or safety standards that affect our community is not a new idea. Great lawyers have always understood that this idea is at the very heart of a civil lawsuit. Watch some of the early videos of the great New York trial lawyer Moe Levine, who died in 1974.[2] Whether presenting a slip-and-fall accident or a medical malpractice claim, the heart of his argument was always community safety and a violation of the rules that protect the community.

More recently, the trial lawyer's Bible for finding the rules and standards that fit your case is the book *Rules of the Road* by attorneys Rick Friedman and Pat Malone. It is a book that every trial lawyer needs to have in his or her library.[3]

---

2. Moe Levine, *The Historic Recordings* (Portland, OR: Trial Guides, 2009); Moe Levine, *The Lost Recordings,* vol. 1 (Portland, OR: Trial Guides 2011); Moe Levine, *The Lost Recordings,* vol. 2 (Portland, OR: Trial Guides, 2012).

3. Rick Friedman and Patrick Malone, *Rules of the Road: A Plaintiff Lawyer's Guide to Proving Liability*, 2nd ed. (Portland, OR: Trial Guides, 2010).

FINDING RULES OR STANDARDS
FOR YOUR CASE

For automobile or trucking accidents, the rules may be embodied in federal or state law, such as statutes or regulations designed to protect the traveling public by prohibiting drunk driving, speeding, or running stop signs. Federal regulations limit the number of hours a trucker can be on the road without a rest break, require the inspection of semitrucks before traveling and at checkpoints, and require daily logbooks that are supposed to record miles and routes traveled.

If there are no laws or statutes prohibiting the conduct in your case, look to the written industry standards, the guidelines, or recommended protocols from associations that regulate the profession's conduct. One example is the nonprofit Joint Commission on Accreditation of Healthcare Organizations (JCAHO), which accredits hospitals. Best of all, find the internal policies and procedures of the relevant organization or governmental entity. It is indefensible hypocrisy for a company to claim it did nothing wrong when its employees violated the company's own written policies or procedures.

Internal Rules or Operating Procedures

In our cases against police or sheriff's departments, the written Standard Operating Procedures (SOPs) have provided the petard upon which the officers have hoisted themselves.

In the case of the "eight-mile lawless zone" where police officers regularly ran stop signs and went up to 112 mph in a 40 mph zone, the sheriff's department's own SOPs provided two basic rules:

◆ Sheriff's officers must obey the law.

◆ Sheriff's officers must enforce the law when they see it violated.

Those rules not only meant that the officers shouldn't speed or run stop signs—which endangers the driving public—but that they should have been citing or reporting fellow officers when they saw them violating those same traffic laws.

Hospital protocols are another example of internal operating procedures. Many hospitals have written protocols requiring that if a patient reports chest pain or discomfort, the medical staff must run an EKG test within ten minutes of that report to determine if the person is having a heart attack. An unnecessary death that results from violating this simple rule designed to save lives through an inexpensive and noninvasive test is inexcusable. In addition to the defendants' own policies and procedures, you can also look for rules in their own training materials, such as PowerPoint slide presentations and videos that they used for training purposes.

In a child's malpractice case, we found a Pediatric Advanced Life Support (PALS) training program for nurses on how to recognize and treat shock in children. A simple PowerPoint slide said treatment should consist of immediate intravenous infusion of "fluids, fluids, fluids." The nurses in our case violated that rule by letting a three-year-old girl with clear signs of shock languish for hours without starting an IV. Providing her immediate and rapid fluids would have saved her life.

Claims from Advertising

Another good source of rules are the promises a company makes in its own advertising on its website, print ads, commercials, promotional materials, and brochures. One valve manufacturing company advertised that it would not only sell its product, but would assist in the design of process systems to make sure they operated safely. From that advertisement we got the company representative to admit the rule that its company should never unnecessarily endanger people by agreeing to install an unsafe valve.

The company broke that advertising promise and rule when it allowed the installation of one of its valves that was not equipped with a backflow preventer into a plant that removed ethane from natural gas. Without a backflow preventer, the valve allowed the highly explosive gas to leak back into the workspace, resulting in a massive explosion that severely burned three men.

In a quest to attract business, companies often advertise that they are "the best" or the "Number 1 Hospital" or are a nursing home that provides "superior care—better than you get at home." All of these are promises that raise the level of care that the public should expect from those organizations.

Rules in Religious Texts

Finally, if all else fails in your quest for a set of rules for your case, you can fall back on the basic moral codes found in religious texts like the Bible, the Koran, and the Torah. There is nothing wrong with using the original Golden Rule as a basis for how the company should have behaved so as to protect the community: "Do unto others as you would have them do unto you."

Where would we find the rules for convenience stores?

6

Rules from the Bloody History of Convenience Stores

Since the day the very first convenience store opened its doors, the industry has been struggling with ways to stop the criminals that convenience stores seemed to attract like flies to honey.

The American convenience store was born in 1927 at the Southland Ice Company in Dallas, Texas. Jefferson Green started selling milk, eggs, and bread from the ice dock on Sundays and after hours, when the regular supermarkets were closed. Inspired by this after-hours business concept, Joe C. Thompson bought the company, turned it into the Southland Corporation, and replaced the ice docks with a series of stand-alone stores that became known as 7-Elevens.

Convenience stores exploded with the rise of the 1950s car culture and expanding suburbs. This new kind of store would be built on the edges of towns, in the burgeoning suburbs or other areas where there was not yet a supermarket. By 1963, the Southland Corporation had one thousand 7-Eleven stores and had started the practice of keeping their stores open all night, rather than only from 7:00 a.m. until 11:00 p.m.

From the day these early convenience stores opened their doors, the business model on which they operated made them instant targets of crime. Built in isolated areas, often on highways or main roads with easy access and escape, the all-night stores were the only place open after the bars closed. For hooligans, drunks, and vampires still on the prowl after midnight, these stores were the only targets available for robbery and other mayhem.

Convenience stores began to be held up so often that police departments around the country came up with a nickname for these new crime hotspots: "Stop and Robs."

How did the convenience store industry respond to this tidal wave of crime?

In 1975, the Southland Corporation hired the Western Behavioral Sciences Institute to study the problem and come up with a set of rules to reduce crime in 7-Eleven stores. The industry-sponsored Southland study came up with a number of low-cost recommendations to reduce crime, including the following security measures:

- Install high-intensity lighting around the perimeter.

- Keep low amounts of cash in the register.

- Train employees on how to react during a robbery.

- Keep windows clear of ads so clerks can see out and police can see in.

- Reduce the escape routes for robbers.

The Southland Corporation implemented these recommendations, and there was a reduction of the crime in its stores. The convenience store industry widely disseminated the Southland research, along with its own research about the most effective standards to prevent crime, to store owners—including the Allsups. Following the first Southland study, numerous government, academic, and other private researchers reported on the phenomenon of late-night retail crime and recommended protecting workers by adding a second clerk, hiring a security guard after dark, closing the stores after dark, adding alarms to alert police, installing security cameras, and placing lone clerks behind bullet-resistant glass enclosures.[1]

Lonnie Allsup acknowledged, "Down through the years, we've always tried to read the National Association of Convenience Stores publications and look at studies and go to seminars, some of my people have."[2] Although informed of these recommendations, the security measures Allsup's usually adopted in its stores were those primarily designed to protect the money or merchandise and which cost little to nothing to adopt. They installed timed drop-safes at a cost of approximately $1,200 each so clerks could keep low amounts of cash in the register, convex mirrors to watch for shoplifters, and inexpensive panic alarm necklaces that were rarely serviced and did not work much of the time.

As an entrepreneur running his own business, Lonnie Allsup decided his company did not need to look for guidance or seek security advice from outside the company about how to reduce crime in his stores. "We, me and my management team, feel that we go through our district managers and that we use our—our own people, management people that we can actually do as well or better than going outside."[3]

When asked whether he had made an effort to learn what kind of security his direct competition, Town and Country Stores, used in 2002, Mr. Allsup responded, "That would not have been

---

1. Department of Criminal Justice Services Virginia Crime Prevention Center, Report to the Virginia State Crime Commission on Violent Crime and Workers' Safety in Virginia Convenience Store (December, 1991); Cal/OSHA, Guidelines for Workplace Security (Revised March 30, 1995); Massachusetts Office of Public Safety, Convenience Store Robbery: A Report of the Incidents, Offenders and Victims of Convenience Store Robbery, Anthony Petrosino and Diana Brensilber (April, 1997); U.S. Department of Labor OSHA, Recommendations for Workplace Violence Prevention Programs in Late-Night Retail Establishments, OSHA 3153 (1998).

2. *McConnell v. Allsup's*, Lonnie Allsup deposition, Vol. I, March 9, 2006, p. 80.

3. *McConnell v. Allsup's*, Lonnie Allsup deposition, Vol. I, March 9, 2006, p. 74.

in my—my job. It would be my operations and my staff."[4] He refused to answer whether the cost of outfitting all three hundred of his stores with video cameras that cost $1,000 to $2,000 each, a total of $300,000 to $600,000 for all stores, was less than his annual salary in 2001.[5]

J.R. Mater, the security expert Allsup's hired before Elizabeth came to work for them, testified that in the 1990s his former employer, Diamond Shamrock, had successfully begun protecting its late-night clerks by placing them in bullet-resistant enclosures after dark. Once a late-night clerk was in the bullet-resistant enclosure, the crime rate dropped to zero. So long as the clerk did not open the door and had access to a phone to call for help, he or she could not be knifed, robbed, raped, or murdered.

The most effective method to reduce crime in convenience stores came out of Gainesville, Florida. In the spring of 1985 in Gainesville, Wayland Clifton, a small-town police chief with tanned, movie-star looks, began studying how to reduce crime in the place where 50 percent of all robberies in the community were taking place: convenience stores. After surveying what other towns had done to solve this problem, his solution was to convince the city to pass an ordinance requiring convenience stores to have two clerks on duty at all times, including the late-night, low-volume, high-crime shift. To Chief Clifton, the solution was as simple as the saying, "there is safety in numbers." If law enforcement officers were trained to have backup in dangerous situations, why wouldn't that same principle work for convenience store clerks?

The convenience store industry howled when Gainesville passed this ordinance. Two clerks on duty at night meant an extra minimum-wage salary and a reduction in profit for these very profitable stores. The industry marshaled all its forces against Chief Clifton. It filed a lawsuit in federal court seeking an injunction to prevent the ordinance from going into effect. They argued that the ordinance would "irreparably harm" the industry by increasing its labor costs and claimed there was no evidence that

4. *Id.*, p. 209.

5. *Id.*, p. 146.

adding an extra clerk would reduce crime. After a hearing, Judge Maurice Paul denied the injunction.

Recognizing that the fight against the convenience store industry was not over and would be carried on in court and into the legislature, Chief Clifton contacted a forensic psychologist, named Dr. Richard Swanson from the University of Florida. Dr. Swanson agreed to conduct a research study into whether adding a second clerk would make a difference in the crime rate in convenience stores. Dr. Swanson undertook the study on the condition that it would be completely independent, that no money would change hands between him and the City of Gainesville, and that the study would be published, regardless of whether it supported Chief Clifton's position.

Dr. Swanson reviewed six years of convenience store crime data, including crime before and after the Gainesville ordinance went into effect on April 2, 1987. He interviewed convenience store robbers about why they selected certain stores to rob, and he interviewed clerks who were victims of robberies about what they thought would have prevented the robberies. The consistent, number-one security measure that made a difference was the presence of more than one clerk on duty.[6] Once the ordinance went into effect, nighttime robberies dropped by 75 percent, proving Chief Clifton's hypothesis. No one murdered or raped a clerk in any Gainesville convenience store after the ordinance went into effect.

Dr. Swanson's study was published, widely disseminated, and discussed in the convenience store industry. Some convenience store chains (like the Town and Country chain in Hobbs) adopted the two-clerk policy. Others, like Allsup's, refused to pay for a second clerk. Instead, Allsup's contributed money to the National Association of Convenience Stores (NACS) to fund their own industry-financed study by sociologist Dr. Rosemary J. Erickson. Dr. Erickson, along with her husband, W.J. Crow,

---

6. Richard Swanson, PsyLaw Institute, "Convenience Store Robbery, A Three Study Approach in 1986 Gainesville, Florida" (presented at the U.S. Department of Labor Conference on Workplace Violence Prevention Programs in High-Risk Late-Night Retail Establishments, Washington, D.C., February 27, 1998).

had been doing industry-sponsored research for years through their Athena Corporation. Unlike Dr. Swanson, Dr. Erickson was paid for her work and, not surprisingly, concluded that despite the Gainesville experience, it was her opinion that a second clerk would not reduce criminal activity. Her studies also discounted other security suggestions that would require the industry to spend money, such as building bullet-resistant enclosures.

After we learned about the research into what security measures worked to reduce crime in convenience stores, we called the experts who were not in the pockets of the industry, Chief Clifton and Dr. Richard Swanson. They agreed to come to New Mexico and testify in our case about the rules and standards that had been proven to reduce convenience store crime.

7

ONE HUNDRED HOURS WORK
FOR EVERY HOUR IN THE
COURTROOM

Three weeks into his summer job with our law firm, a young law student asked for a meeting with me.

After I closed my office door, he said that the job was not working out the way he thought it should. Instead of doing exciting things like arguing in a courtroom or cross-examining a witness, he had been assigned projects like ordering police reports from around the state, doing Internet research on an expert witness for a corporate defendant, and reading through medical records to create a summary of a client's care in a new medical malpractice case. This kind of work just wasn't what he thought he was signing up for.

Having based his decision to apply to our firm after seeing an hour-long demonstration of an opening statement, this young man was not alone in his misconception about the real work of a plaintiffs' lawyer.

Real Law Isn't Like TV

Many young people growing up today are only exposed to the "workplace" through television sitcoms like *The Office*, places where no one ever really works, but everyone spends their time joking around or creating conflict and drama. While this makes for good television, it does not make for good lawyering.

It's not just television that creates this misperception. It exists even among lawyers who represent institutions rather than individuals. I can't tell you how many times I've had an institutional or insurance lawyer tell me how easy I have it because all I have to do is wait until someone walks into my office who has been seriously injured or had a family member killed, then write a demand letter and suddenly money falls out of the sky.

It's never worked that way.

We Do Our Own Investigation

Other lawyers have this misperception because police departments investigate before the case files ever hit the prosecutors' desks. Insurance adjusters investigate cases for insurance defense lawyers. Plaintiffs' lawyers have to figure out what they need and do the investigation themselves. Even in auto accident cases where we may start with a police report, we have to re-interview all the witnesses, visit the scene to preserve evidence, do our own scene reconstruction, and find people the police never interviewed—all on our own.

In one case where a police officer's wife had run a red light and collided with our client, police told the key eyewitness she could leave without being interviewed. Uncomfortable with the investigating officer's failure to even take down her name and contact information, the witness dropped a card with her name and phone number into our client's purse as she was being rolled away on a stretcher to the ambulance. When our client found the card in her purse in the hospital after her damaged kidney was removed, she passed it on to us, and we tracked down this eyewitness. She confirmed our client's account that it was the police officer's wife who had run the red light, not our client. Not surprisingly, having shooed away the eyewitness, the police report had come to the opposite conclusion.

For every hour a jury sees in the courtroom, a good plaintiffs' lawyer and her team has spent one hundred hours outside the courtroom finding the information, synthesizing the evidence, and creating a simple, compelling presentation of the story. The hard truth is that it takes a lot of time and work to build a solid foundation for a concise and powerful story.

The French mathematician Blaise Pascal famously recognized in a letter he wrote in 1657, "I would have written a shorter letter, but I did not have the time."[1]

The same is true of the law. The more time you spend and the more effort you expend in preparation, the shorter and more effective your presentation to the jury will be.

HARD WORK BRINGS LUCK

This was the lesson I learned from one of my own role models, New Mexico's first woman Supreme Court Justice, Mary Walters. A legend in our state, she began her professional life as a transport pilot in the Women's Air Force during World War II, where she learned to drink whiskey and curse with the best of them. With her short-cropped curly hair, she had a quick wit and a spine of burnished steel. Attending law school on the G.I. Bill, she was the only woman in her class. After nine years practicing law, she became the first woman district judge in the state, later ascending to the Court of Appeals and then the New Mexico Supreme Court.

Before we became friends, this remarkable woman came to talk to my law school class. After her lecture, inspired by all she had accomplished, I found the nerve to push through the throng surrounding her. When there was an opening, I breathlessly asked

---

1. Blaise Pascal, "Letter XVI, 4 December, 1656," in *The Provincial Letters*, trans. A. J. Krailsheimer (Penguin Classics, 1982).

her a question born of the same inexperience as my disgruntled summer clerk, "What was the secret of your success in the law?"

She smiled, her eyes twinkling, and spoke only two words. "Hard work," she said. It was the most honest and valuable advice I ever got about practicing law. There was no magic oratory, special power suit, or precise hand gestures that would make me a great trial lawyer. It was all in how I prepared my cases.

"Wait a second," you might be saying to yourself, "I'm not sure I want to work that hard, particularly if I want to have a family, a spouse, or a life outside the law."

You can have all those things and be a trial lawyer too.

Having a Life as a Trial Lawyer

My daughter, Heather McGinn, has always had perfect timing. She was born one day before I was set to take the three-day bar examination to become a lawyer, luckily a day earlier than my official due date. After an amazingly short four-hour labor, there she was at 10:00 a.m. on Sunday morning, her brown eyes bright and already interested in the world.

The hospital wouldn't let us leave for at least eight hours after she was born. They had to make sure she was healthy, and they wanted me to rest, which is why the nurses kept coming in and taking away my study materials until I had to hide them under my pillow.

After a night at home with my precious new daughter, during which I was so excited about her birth I could not sleep, I showed up to take the test at 8:00 a.m. This was only made possible because of a large pillow I sat on during the test and my mother, Jean McGinn, who drove up to Albuquerque from Las Cruces to watch Heather. She, my father, and my husband would bring the baby to the exam site over the lunch hour to breastfeed.

When the results of the bar exam came out and I had passed, it was not a sign of any superpower on my part. Once Heather was born, all the pressure to pass or fail was lifted from my shoulders. I knew that if I flunked, no one would blame me. Any failure would be chalked up to having given birth right before the test. In fact, with all the leftover adrenaline and other pregnancy hormones coursing through my body from delivering a baby, I probably had a chemical advantage over the other test-takers.

I didn't have the luxury of choosing whether to work or not, and so went to work at my first job as a lawyer six weeks after Heather was born. Unrelated to the job, I was divorced and a single mom by the time she was one year old. So began the conundrum all single working parents—including Elizabeth Garcia—face. How do you balance your life when you want to have it all?

Balancing Life and Work

The answer is that you can have it all. You just can't have it all at the same time. There is no "balance" in the full-to-the-brim life of a working mother. To accomplish all you need to do, some days you short your children, some days you short your job, some days you short your spouse or partner. Always, you short yourself. And, when your children are small, you never get enough sleep.

I started my most intense job right after my divorce, when my daughter was one year old. I became a violent crimes prosecutor with the Bernalillo County District Attorney's Office. This meant a huge but fascinating caseload of important cases and an average of fifteen trials a year.

For the next three years of my life, my weekday schedule was to wake up at 6:00 or 7:00 a.m. to feed my daughter breakfast, get her ready, and take her to day care or preschool. I would be at work or in court from 8:00 a.m. until 5:00 p.m. At the start of any trial, I would let the judge know we could not work late because I had to pick up my daughter no later than 5:30 and that there was no one else to do it. The judge would often announce to the jury that this was the reason we had to stop at 5:00 p.m.

After picking Heather up by 5:30 p.m., we would have dinner, play, and talk. I would give her a bath, read her a book, and put her to bed by 9:00 p.m. In this time before laptop computers and the Internet, I hired a babysitter to come in to watch her after she was asleep, allowing me to go back to the office where I would usually work until 2:00 or 3:00 a.m. getting ready for trial or catching up on my cases. Then I would come home and catch three or four hours of sleep before the cycle started all over again.

If you think this is an extraordinary schedule, you are not a working mother who has small children. Women do what they have to do. Single fathers do the same.

Trial and Parenting Small Children

All of my law partners had children after coming to work for our firm. Because we understood what that meant, the other non-pregnant women all stepped up to cover for the one who was figuring out how to fit in all she had to do, with a newborn or small child at home.

When we went to trial in Elizabeth Garcia's case, my law partner Elicia Montoya's daughter, Sienna, was just eight months old, and Elicia was still breastfeeding. In the small Santa Fe courthouse, there was no private room for Elicia to pump her breast milk during trial. This meant, on breaks, she had to go to the corner in the back of the courtroom to set up the machine and pump what she could.

This led to an embarrassing moment for our male opposing counsel. Ignoring the "scree, scree" sound of the machine and the fact that Elicia's back was turned to him, he came rushing up to her with a question, despite her saying she was busy and couldn't answer right now. Poking his head around her shoulder, his eyes got really wide; he stopped his question in mid-sentence and rushed off. I don't think he spoke to Elicia again for the rest of the case.

Keep the Dream, Give Up the Guilt

Don't give up the dream of having it all. Instead, give up the guilt of not being Martha-Stewart-perfect. Good male lawyers will work just as hard as you; they just won't feel guilty about it. As soon as you can afford it, hire someone to help clean your house. Buy, don't bake, the healthy food you're required to bring for your child's snack day.

Find a partner or spouse who understands and appreciates the work you do outside the home. Fortunately, the love of my life for the last twenty-five years, Charles Daniels (no, I did not make him change his name after we were married), was himself a criminal defense lawyer who understood the intensity of preparing for and being in trial. He knew that when I stayed late at the office I wasn't cheating or having fun somewhere without him, but was preparing for trial. Nothing will help you like a partner who is proud of you and supports your success.

Don't Be Afraid to Work Hard

Don't be afraid of hard work. The harder you work, the luckier you will get in the courtroom. When you see a lawyer appear to pull a rabbit out of a hat in the courtroom, it is because he or she has done the work outside the courtroom to line up thirty other rabbits in hats and was just hoping for an opening to use one of them. If you are not willing to put in the seat-time and shoe leather doing the investigation, Internet searches, massive record-review, research, and discovery necessary to put together a case, then you, like the plaintive, disappointed young law clerk, need to find another job.

Elizabeth Garcia's case was an exception to the one-hundred-hour rule. Because the Allsups fought us on every discovery request and rarely produced any of the information we sought in discovery, including the crime reports we needed to prove our case, we had to spend two hundred hours of work for every hour in the courtroom.

8

LIFE ON THE FRONT LINES OF AN ALLSUP'S CONVENIENCE STORE

Allegra Carpenter, Kathy Love, Elicia Montoya, and Randi McGinn
Photo by Kip Malone

The two hundred hours of work for every hour in the courtroom in Elizabeth Garcia's case began with our effort to find out how bad the crime problem really was in Allsup's convenience stores. My law partners, Allegra Carpenter, Elicia Montoya, and Kathy Love, undertook this massive project and put together a team of young women who spent almost two years finding all the police reports for Allsup's locations in New Mexico, Texas, and Oklahoma.

The work of our young law clerk, Katie Curry, was so impressive we hired her as an associate when she graduated from law school. After helping us track down and sort through thousands of crime reports, college students Juliet Keene and Ana Romero Jurrison both went on to law school after they finished their undergraduate degrees. We also were fortunate to have an all-hands-on-deck support staff who pitched in to help, including assistant Jane Baskerville, paralegals Chris Papaleo and Roberta Trujillo, tech expert Sean O'Neill, receptionist Darla Perea, law clerk Juliana Koob, and our office manager, Lorraine Martinez. In trying to ferret out the truth in a case, it helps to have a big dose of dogged persistence in your DNA. The people you are coming after never make it easy for you to find out what is really going on inside their businesses.

Once you file a lawsuit, the discovery rules technically allow you to ask questions and obtain documents from the other side. Good, ethical defense lawyers stand up to their clients and require them to produce even damaging information requested in discovery. Other lawyers, or those who need the business, end up in thrall to their corporate clients and spend all their time finding creative ways not to answer your questions or produce any of the documents you need.

The first two lawyers for Allsup's Convenience Stores Inc. were Chris Key, a local Albuquerque lawyer, and Phil Kreihbel, a lawyer who had recently returned from a several-year sabbatical and was trying to rebuild his practice. They fought us on everything we requested, from a simple list of all the Allsup's stores in New Mexico, Texas, and Oklahoma to the financial records showing the income from the Allsup's stores in Hobbs. Even after the judge ordered them to produce the requested information, these lawyers claimed Allsup's no longer had any records that were responsive to our requests. This claim would come back to haunt them at trial, when the judge wouldn't let them introduce the records they "found" right before trial and wanted to introduce in our case.

ALLSUP'S HISTORY OF VIOLENCE

DATE	CITY	ST	M/F clerk	3RD shift	DESCRIPTION OF ACTS
2/5/75	Clovis	NM			• Female clerk alone on 3rd shift • **Abducted, raped, sodomized, murdered** • **Clerk brutally beaten, skull fractured**
6/5/76	Plainview	TX			• Female clerk alone on 3rd shift • **Strong arm** robbery and **assault** • no permanent injuries.
12/6/76	Lorenzo	TX			• Female clerk alone on 3rd shift • **Armed assailant pointed a revolver at the clerk, pushed her to the ground, broke her wrist, then threw her toward cash register**
4/19/77	Eunice	NM			• Female clerk alone on 3rd shift • **Armed robbery: shotgun**
12/4/77	Plainview	TX			• Female clerk alone on 3rd shift • **Armed robbery: gun**
1/7/78	Pampa	TX			• Female clerk alone on 3rd shift • **Armed robbery: gun** • Assailant pointed a gun in clerk's face, then stepped toward her.
3/30/78	Plainview	TX			• Female clerk alone on 3rd shift • **Armed robbery: gun** • Assailant pointed gun at clerk
7/13/78	Plainview	TX			• Female clerk alone on 3rd shift • **Armed robbery; gun and tire iron; 2 assailants** • **Assailants forced clerk to the floor**
7/28/78	Kress	TX			• Female clerk alone on 3rd shift • **Armed robbery: gun and tire iron; 2 assailants** • **Assailant hit clerk over the head with tire iron, knocking him out.**
8/30/78	Groom	TX			• Female clerk alone on 3rd shift • Robbery/Assault; 2 assailants • Assailant **shoved and pinned** clerk to the floor.
10/8/78	Kress	TX			• Female clerk alone on 3rd shift • Armed robbery: gun; 2 assailants

PLAINTIFF'S
EXHIBIT
11

Page 1 of 93

An exhibit we created for trial based on our research[1]

1. This illustration shows only one page of this report. The full report, called "Report Allsups History of Violence," is available at http://www.trialguides.com/resources/downloads/changing-laws.

The most problematic "missing" information were the records we requested of all criminal activity, including robberies, beatings, rapes, and murders, in Allsup's stores. They claimed not to have such records, and said they did not know how many clerks had been killed on duty during the thirty years the stores had been in operation. We needed this information to prove that Allsup's knew about the danger to the lone clerks who worked in its stores.

In attempting to hide the information we needed, Allsup's did not count on that great equalizer and fount of all information in the modern era—the Internet. With a combination of Internet and phone book searches, we were able to find every Allsup's store in the three-state area—all 310 of them, with town and street addresses.

Once we located all the stores, we spent the next year sending letters to every police department in the towns where these stores were located, asking for police reports of crimes at every one of the 310 store addresses for the last five years. With a little follow-up and prompting, the reports began flooding in—so many that we decided to pull out all of the minor crimes like shoplifting or people who drove off without paying for gas.

After two years of work, we had a stack of binders filled with 1,225 police reports, each one telling the story of an Allsup's clerk who was terrorized in an armed robbery, beaten, raped, or murdered. We compiled these reports in a summary with icons indicating whether the attacks were at night, whether they involved a single clerk, and whether the clerk was male or female.

From the huge heap of misery contained in these reports, we found witnesses, mostly former clerks or their family members, who were willing to share their stories and testify at trial. Among the families of the thirteen clerks murdered while working in an Allsup's, we found two families willing to tell us about the broken promises Allsup's had made to them. We also found one clerk who survived an assault.

Sixteen years before Elizabeth Garcia ever went to work for Allsup's, Eva Pellissier, another young mother with four kids, went to work at an Allsup's, also in Hobbs. Like Elizabeth, she was scheduled to work the graveyard shift alone, without any security

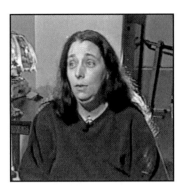

Eva Pellissier

devices. On the night of August 31, 1986, three men came into the store where Eva was working and robbed her. Although she gave them everything in the cash register, the men took a knife and cut her throat from ear to ear. Eva fell to the floor and pretended to be dead until the men left the store.

When they were gone, Eva grabbed a dirty glove she had been using to stock shelves, covered her throat, and tried to use the phone that was behind the counter. It didn't work. She crawled to the house next door, but no one was home. She then crawled back to the store and saw some change on the ground that she picked up and used in the outside payphone to dial 911. Though she could barely make audible sounds through her torn throat, she was able to get through, and the dispatcher sent an ambulance to the store.

While Eva was in the emergency room of the hospital, the local Allsup's district manager came to her bedside. He was standing there when the doctor came in with a pencil and paper to ask her to put in writing what she wanted to happen with her children. The doctor told Eva that because she had lost so much blood, she was probably not going to make it.

The district manager told Eva he was so sorry and asked if there was anything he could do for her. Taking his hand in her own and looking him right in the eyes, Eva croaked out her last request.

"Please," she said, "you swear to me that you will never put another woman on the graveyard shift alone."

Holding her gaze, the Allsup's district manager promised her that no woman would ever work alone on the graveyard shift again.[1]

Luckily, the doctor was wrong. After a fifteen-hour surgery to put her throat back together and insert a tracheotomy tube, Eva Pellissier survived. She had to use the trach tube for about a year and a half and was so affected by post-traumatic stress disorder that she never went back to work for Allsup's again. The one thought that gave her comfort was that Allsup's had promised to fix the problem. It was that promise that caused her to settle out her workers' compensation and not engage in litigation.

Imagine her surprise when, sixteen years later, she learned of the death of a lone female clerk in her hometown. Allsup's had never kept its promise. Eva Pellissier was not only willing to help us, she would be our first witness at trial, rasping out her story, the scar on her neck still visible above the collar of her blouse.

Eva was not alone in her willingness to help out. Through our search of police records, we also found the family of Amanda Rockford.[2] A single mother with two children, thirty-one-year-old Amanda went to work at an Allsup's store in Santa Fe, New Mexico—eleven years before Eva Pellissier had her throat cut and twenty-seven years before Elizabeth Garcia was killed.

In 1975, Amanda was working alone on the graveyard shift in a store with no security. A drunken stranger on the way home from a bar after 2:00 a.m. spotted her working by herself with no one else around. The man took her from the store, raped her, beat her to death, and left her partially clothed body in an isolated parking lot.

On the day of her funeral, the owner of the company, Lonnie Allsup, stopped by the home of Amanda Rockford's mother.

---

1. *McConnell v. Allsup's*, Eva Pellissier affidavit. A full copy of this affidavit, called "Affidavit Eva Pellissier," is available at http://www.trialguides.com/resources/downloads/changing-laws.

2. At the family's request, we have changed the names and some of the identifying details of this story. Throughout this book, Amanda Rockford and Robert Christiansen are pseudonyms for a murdered Allsup's employee and her brother.

After offering his condolences, Mr. Allsup asked her if there was anything he could do. "Yes," said Amanda's mother. "Whatever you do, never leave a woman alone on the graveyard shift in one of your stores."

There in the family living room in 1975, Lonnie Allsup promised Amanda Rockford's mother that he would no longer let women work alone on the graveyard shift. Although Amanda's mother was deceased by the time we found this family, there was a witness to this promise. Standing in the living room at the time was Amanda's teenage brother, Robert Christiansen. Robert had been so affected by his sister's death that he became a law enforcement officer. He was appalled that Allsup's had never kept its promise to his mother, and agreed to be a witness in our trial.

Our third broken promise came from the family of John Deibler. At the time of his death, John was forty-three and a married man with two teenage children. John worked alone on the graveyard shift in an Allsup's store in Ruidoso, New Mexico.

On August 29, 1998—four years before Elizabeth Garcia was murdered—two people came in after the bars closed to rob the store of some beer. The thieves ordered John Deibler into the cooler, where they stabbed him twenty-seven times and left him dead in a pool of his own blood. Because there were no security cameras in the store, the killers were never caught.

On the day of John's funeral, it was the son and Allsup's manager, Mark Allsup, who came to the Deibler home. Just like his father had done over twenty years before with Amanda Rockford's mother, Mark Allsup asked Angela Deibler whether there was anything he could do.

"Yes," said Angela Deibler. "Please do what the other convenience stores have already done and install security cameras in your stores. It might have prevented John's death and would have helped the police catch the people who killed my husband."[3]

In 1998, Mark Allsup promised Angela Deibler that the company would install cameras in its stores. Four years later, when

---

3. *McConnell v. Allsup's*, Angela Deibler testimony. This is a paraphrase of Angela Deibler's testimony.

Elizabeth Garcia came to work at Allsup's, Mark had not kept that promise. There were no security cameras in most Allsup's stores in New Mexico, including the Ruidoso store where John Deibler was killed.

Angela Deibler agreed to be a witness at trial. She would testify about how she did not pursue any legal action against Allsup's because she believed the company would keep its promise and protect future workers with security cameras. Something that she now realized Allsup's had never done.

In addition to the three families Allsup's had placated with broken promises, Allegra found, and obtained sworn affidavits from, a group of people who had worked at Allsup's stores in Hobbs before Elizabeth was hired. Some Anglo, some Hispanic, some African American, both men and women, the workers were a cross section of those American workers across the nation who struggle to support their families on minimum wage.

Lensdale Cordice was robbed at knifepoint and severely beaten by two men at 1:30 a.m. while working alone on the graveyard shift in Allsup's Store No. 3. He talked about how "a lot of the people who came into the store at night on the graveyard shift were very scary. They were lunatic and psycho-looking." Even though he was a man, he said, "You feel especially vulnerable at night because there is no traffic at night and fewer normal people coming into the store."[4]

Theresa Garcia was hired as an Allsup's manager trainee in 2001. On December 1, 2001, she was robbed at knifepoint while working alone on the graveyard shift. She had been given no training on what to do in a robbery. There were no security cameras in her store. The lighting outside was broken and absent, and when she pressed the necklace alarm she had been given, it did not work.

Her manager, Debra Carr, did not seem concerned about her, but was concerned that she had not "made a drop to lower the cash in the drawer" below the $50 limit. In Ms. Garcia's words, "They were upset that so much money had been stolen." The amount taken was $70. After the robbery, Ms. Garcia requested

4. *McConnell v. Allsup's*, Lensdale Cordice affidavit.

to be moved to the day shift. When a week went by and she was still being assigned to the graveyard shift, she quit because she was afraid for her own safety.[5]

Before Elizabeth was killed, Allsup's worker Thelma Barber asked her manager why employees were forced to work alone on the graveyard shift and requested a second worker and security cameras. Her request was turned down. Within a day or two after Elizabeth was abducted, three "high-up Allsup's managers" came to Hobbs. During that meeting, Thelma said, "I asked the high-up managers if we could have a second person on staff. They said, 'No.' I asked if the stores could have security cameras and I was told that the revenues coming out of the Hobbs district did not warrant the installation of security cameras. Insufficient revenues was the only explanation that I was given for Allsup's refusal to provide additional security in the stores, even after Elizabeth Garcia's abduction."[6]

Sylvia Chidester was forced to work alone on the graveyard shift at several Allsup's locations in Hobbs. There were times when she was so scared she was shaking. After her manager denied her request to schedule a second person to work with her, she asked her husband Sam to come and stay in the store to protect her, even though he was not getting paid for his time. Her request to increase the lighting in the store was also denied, and she testified that the necklace alarms provided by Allsup's did not work most of the time because the batteries were often dead.

Ms. Chidester was the person who showed Elizabeth Garcia the ropes during the week she spent training at Store No. 145, before she was assigned to work alone on the graveyard shift at Store No. 146 on the Lovington Highway. "Elizabeth told me she didn't like working after dark, but I told her there was very little I could do about it." After Elizabeth was murdered and nothing changed at the Allsup's stores, Ms. Chidester quit because she was so nervous.[7]

---

5. *McConnell v. Allsup's*, Theresa Garcia affidavit.

6. *McConnell v. Allsup's*, Thelma Barber affidavit.

7. *McConnell v. Allsup's*, Sylvia Chidester affidavit.

Finally there was Harvey Price, who worked in management for Allsup's from 1994 to 2000, including as the Area Supervisor over the Hobbs stores. Price stated the following in his affidavit:

> Hobbs Allsup's were an extremely dangerous place for clerks to work. As an Area Supervisor, I did not regularly work in the stores, but in an emergency, such as when a clerk had been robbed or injured and needed to go home, to the police station, or the hospital, I would occasionally take over a shift. I always feared for my life to work a graveyard shift in a Hobbs store.
>
> I felt guilty about hiring people to work at Allsup's knowing that they would be exposed to extreme danger working alone on the graveyard shift. I was extremely concerned for their safety, yet there was nothing I could do about it. While Allsup's felt that the Hobbs stores were profitable enough to keep open, Allsup's did not deem them profitable enough to warrant any investment in security or employee safety.[8]

The lawyers in my office, along with our paralegals, assistants, and staff, would not have found any of these witnesses without the countless hours they spent outside the courtroom. These were just some of the rabbits in hats that we lined up and got ready to use. Through our efforts, we had located the heroes and heroines in our case.

---

8. *McConnell v. Allsup's*, Harvey Price affidavit.

9

HEROES AND HEROINES

In movies and literature, Americans have a broad range of people we accept as heroes or heroines. In fiction, we are disdainful of those who are truly innocent, naïve, or pure as the driven snow. We like our heroes and heroines, particularly our action heroes, a little dirty. Think of all the flawed antiheroes we root for on film, television, or in novels: Dexter Morgan, a serial killer who kills serial killers; Michael Corleone from *The Godfather;* Jason Stratham's unnamed character in *The Transporter;* Ellen Ripley in the *Alien* movies; Butch Cassidy and the Sundance Kid; and Clint Eastwood in virtually every movie he's ever done.

CAN THE CLIENT BE THE HERO OR HEROINE?

While antiheroes make for great drama, jurors are less forgiving of flawed clients—the first place you look in your case for a hero. Some prospective clients' past acts, in varying degrees, will cause the jury to not believe them or to find against them on liability despite the facts. Even if you win on liability, the clients' flaws will affect the amount of damages the jury will award. This is the problematic unnamed factor you won't find in any jury instruction. The jury wants to know that your client deserves the money. In a civil lawsuit, even if your clients looked as good as the youthful Paul Newman and Robert Redford, it would be difficult for a jury to award Butch and Sundance a large verdict.

If your plan is to use your client as the hero or heroine of your case, at an appropriate moment early on, find out whether there are any minefields ahead. This conversation is a difficult one to have in your first meeting, while you are still building the trust you will need to get through the long litigation process. Once trust is established, you should explain to your client that you can only protect him or her if you know where the dangers lie. You should find out the following, in descending order of concern:

Client Flaw	Potential Effect on the Case
Involved in Other Lawsuits	Of all the flaws your client can have, this is one of the most worrisome. Some jurors, taken in by insurance and business industry marketing, may use this to make a snap judgment about your client being one of those mythical people who file "frivolous" lawsuits and is just hoping to hit the lottery in this case.
Undocumented Workers	The way most jurors view this problem is that your client is in this country illegally and should not benefit in any way from the American legal system.
Prior Criminal Conviction	Depending on the type of conviction and the length of time that has passed since it occurred, this can be a big problem for your case. Crimes involving fraud are a concern if you need the jury to believe your client's testimony. The more serious the crime, the more frequent the convictions, and the closer in time to the case, the harder it will be to make your client the hero in your case.

CLIENT FLAW	POTENTIAL EFFECT ON THE CASE
Mental Illness	Mental illness scares jurors, even if you explain that it is a disease process for which the person should not bear any blame. If the mental illness is one that results in violence or threatening outbursts, it is even more difficult to make your client the hero or heroine of your case.
Not Filing Tax Returns	The client's failure to pay taxes, when all of the jurors have contributed to support the community, is particularly troubling to jurors, especially when it comes to damages.
Bankruptcy	A bankruptcy makes jurors wonder why they should award any money. If the client couldn't handle his or her finances before, the jury may be concerned he or she will just blow it again.
Drug or Alcohol Abuse	Surprisingly, unless your client was under the influence at the time he or she was hurt, jurors more readily forgive this problem, particularly if it was in the past and your client has worked to overcome the drug or alcohol problem. Many courts will keep this out of evidence if not directly related to the case facts.
Unmarried Parents	Given that as of 2012, more than 40 percent of all births in the United States are to unmarried mothers, the stigma of this former bugaboo has lessened in all but the most conservative jury venues.

A flaw or problem with your client doesn't necessarily mean you turn down the case, just that you may not be able to feature the client as the hero or heroine. Remember: flaws are what make us human, interesting, and different from each other. There are ways to explain and help the jury understand all but the most horrible of human foibles.

OTHER PEOPLE WHO CAN BE THE HERO OR

HEROINE

If you can't use your client as the hero or heroine of the case, there are others who can fill this role. The following are some examples of real heroes and heroines from real cases:

- The whistleblower who testifies about discriminatory practices in a corporate office.

- The neighbor who comes forward to report what she saw through the fence when police officers shot an unarmed man in his own backyard.

- The nurse's aide who quit her job at a nursing home after being asked to fill in blanks in patient charts to cover up that the residents were not receiving required care because of short staffing.

And, of course, the best heroes and heroines possible in every case are the jurors themselves.[1] It is the jurors alone who have the power to right the wrongs committed in the case and to make the community safer through their verdict. The role of the jurors is so important that they have their own chapter later in the book.[2]

In addition to the parade of minimum-wage workers who had already risked their lives alone on the graveyard shift in Allsup's stores, we were able to find an unlikely pair of heroes in Elizabeth Garcia's case.

---

1. For an entire book on how to turn your jurors into the heroes of the case, I highly recommend Carl Bettinger's *Twelve Heroes, One Voice* (Portland, OR: Trial Guides, 2011).

2. See chapter 23, "Finding Courageous Jurors to Be the Heroes and Heroines of Your Case."

10

A Hero and an Antihero Arise

There were heroes and heroines aplenty in Elizabeth Garcia's case. The list started with Elizabeth Garcia herself, the single mother who was trying to make a better life for her family. It included all of the Allsup's clerks who over the years had worked alone at night for minimum wage to support themselves and their families, and had been robbed, beaten, raped, and murdered.

The two men who would become a centerpiece of our case were on opposite ends of the hero spectrum. One was a cop and one was a crook.

The cop was Hobbs Chief of Police Tony Knott. Chief Knott was the kind of conscientious and caring person that any small town would be lucky to have enforcing the law. He took his job of protecting and serving the citizens who had hired him seriously. Reducing crime in Hobbs was his first priority. He obtained funding for a database to input all the crime data for the town of Hobbs so he could track crime trends. After inputting all the crime data for the city, Chief Knott made a surprising discovery. Most of the crime in the city of Hobbs was occurring at Allsup's convenience store locations: "From 1998 to 2002 there were forty-nine felonies committed at the eight Allsup's stores in Hobbs compared to eight or nine [at the Town and Country stores]."[1]

Chief Knott visited all the stores in both chains to try and figure out why one was a crime magnet and the other was not. The difference? Chief Knott testified in his deposition:

> It wasn't a matter for us that the Allsup's are in areas that are more prone to crime and Town and Country stores are not, that is just not true. They both have stores all over town . . . but in the Town and Country stores there were always surveillance camera systems [something 89 percent of convenience stores nationally had by 2000] . . . we [the Hobbs police] didn't spend much time at Town and Country stores. We spent a huge amount of time at Allsup's stores. We saw that the Town and Country stores were much better lit than the Allsup's stores. They tended to have fewer obstructions on their windows . . . Town and Country stores seemed to train their employees and where Allsup's stores . . . my gut was that maybe they weren't receiving any kind of training . . . Over the years, typically, Town and Country will have two people in their stores at night. And Allsup's typically had one person in their store. You know, it is pretty difficult . . . to rape and abduct a woman when there are two of them versus one.[2]

After completing his analysis, Chief Knott put together his statistical research and his findings and asked for a meeting with Allsup's acting president, son Mark Allsup. His presentation was simple. He told Mark Allsup he had found a way to make both of them successful, by protecting Allsup's employees and reducing crime in the City of Hobbs.

---

1. *McConnell v. Allsup's*, Tony Knott deposition, p. 27.

2. *McConnell v. Allsup's*, Tony Knott deposition, p. 25–27.

I ended up talking with Mark Allsup . . . I explained the process by which we had determined that statistically [Allsup's crime was greater than Town and Country] . . . and we felt we had an easy solution. I didn't get a positive response at all . . . it was rather arrogant. [He said], "We're not going to do that. We're not interested in that, and frankly, there is not one thing you can do about that." He was right. I mean, all I could do was ask. I couldn't make him put video cameras in his store.[3]

Chief Knott was stunned by the angry reaction. Before leaving, he had these words for Mark Allsup:

If we don't resolve this problem, if we don't make these stores safer, we're going to be talking about a murder. Somebody is going to be murdered at one of your stores and it is just a tragic shame that you wouldn't take, you know, just the minimum, just the bare minimum of steps to keep that from—prevent that from happening.[4]

This prescient conversation took place one year before Elizabeth Garcia went to work on the graveyard shift at an Allsup's store in Hobbs. The day they found her body in the abandoned lot, Chief Knott told the local paper, "I warned Allsup's this was going to happen."[5]

When asked in his deposition what his first thought was when he learned of the death, Chief Knott testified:

I was furious. I wasn't throwing things or hollering. Not like that, but my first thought was, you know,

3. *McConnell v. Allsup's*, Tony Knott deposition, p. 33, 35–38.

4. *McConnell v. Allsup's*, Tony Knott deposition, p. 42.

5. Mark R. Fletcher, "Convenience store security law," *Hobbs News-Sun*, January 19, 2002.

this is outrageous . . . why hadn't Allsup's heeded my warning and tried to resolve the problem before this happened? Here we had a young mother who was brutally, brutally slain. She was slaughtered like an animal and left out in the field and I kind of take that personal, because it was my responsibility to keep those kinds of things from happening. I took it very personally, and it was just outrageous that it happened.[6]

By the time we found and interviewed Chief Knott, he had retired from the Hobbs Police Department and, shortly thereafter, was diagnosed with terminal cancer. Like all witnesses, he had a choice when we spoke to him. He could keep quiet about his encounter with this powerful southern New Mexico business and avoid any political repercussions or he could tell us the truth about how he had tried to protect his community. Real heroes are not just made on the battlefield, but in the everyday decisions we make to either avoid discomfort in our own lives or help others by telling the truth. He chose to tell the truth. Although we preserved his testimony with a videotaped deposition, he survived until trial and was able to testify in person to the jury.

Brian Nash

On the other end of the spectrum was our crook, Brian Nash. One of the few African American kids in Hobbs, Brian had been

6. *McConnell v. Allsup's*, Tony Knott deposition, p. 43.

a high school football star. During the summer between his graduation from high school and college, unable to find a job, he began robbing Allsup's stores.

Brian never used a weapon and never hurt anybody. It was so easy; he began using the stores like a bank, dropping in for cash about once a week. As he testified (when we located him in prison), because there were no security cameras, he would never have been caught if he hadn't gotten greedy and tried to rob three Allsup's stores in one night. On that night, Chief Knott's Hobbs police officers were waiting for him when he showed up at the third store.

My law partner Allegra Carpenter traveled down to the Lea County Correctional Facility where Brian Nash was serving his sentence for the Allsup's robberies. She took a videographer to record a videotape deposition of Brian Nash. Brian became an expert witness of sorts on what robbers look for in choosing a vulnerable target.

Brian Nash testified that he selected Allsup's to rob over and over again because the stores looked like easy pickings. The stores had poor lighting, particularly in the dark parking lot, where he could wait unseen until the store was empty of customers. The posters in the windows obscured the clerk's view of him lurking outside. At night, the store was staffed with only one clerk, usually a woman, who would be easy to intimidate. Finally, there was no way to get caught because there were no video cameras in the store.

In his career as a convenience store robber, Brian never held up any of the Town and Country stores because there were always two clerks, there were always security cameras, and the stores "were lit up like a Christmas tree."[7]

Why did we consider Brian Nash a hero, in our case? He did not need to help us with this invaluable insight into the mind of a robber. He could have asserted his constitutional Fifth Amendment right to stay silent. Instead, he helped the jury understand why the Allsup's stores were attractive targets for criminals. Brian Nash was a true redemption story. After being released from prison in 2011, he returned to his Christian faith and to Hobbs where he got a job, got married, and is now the

---

7. *McConnell v. Allsup's*, Brian Nash deposition.

father of a three-year-old son. He redeemed himself through his truthful testimony and by serving prison time for the series of youthful indiscretions that scared but never harmed any Allsup's employee. The same could not be said of the villains we discovered in the case.

11

Uncovering the Villains in Your Case

Great movies and great literature have great villains. Some you know are evil and nefarious from the start. Hannibal Lecter is so dangerous that when we see him for the first time, he is locked behind a seemingly impenetrable cage and later wears a mask to prevent him from taking a bite out of a woman senator's throat. Sonorous, mouth-breathing Darth Vader radiates evil. Sauron, the antagonist in J.R.R. Tolkien's *Lord of the Rings*, is described as an all-seeing evil eye with an insatiable lust for the power of the one ring that will bind them all.

Some villains seem benevolent at the beginning and reveal themselves over time as the proverbial wolf in sheep's clothing, like Norman Bates, the helpful clerk who checks you in at the Bates motel. Napoleon the pig in George Orwell's *Animal Farm* claims to act out of his concern for the community of animals, but once he seizes power, he extracts false confessions and executes those who oppose his will. Others are masters at manipulation and deception, like Shakespeare's Iago, who tricks Othello into killing his own wife by falsely convincing him she is having an affair. It is these betrayers of trust that are doomed to the ice of Dante's lowest circle of Hell.

Villains Are Selfish

All villains have one thing in common: self-interest drives them—whether it is greed, a lust for power, murderous anger, or the unfettered hedonistic pleasure of doing whatever they want, just because they can. The worse the villain, the better your case is.

The scariest villains are those whose selfish acts threaten our own survival or endanger our family in some way. It is this villain—the monster who may eat us—that activates the alarms in the most primitive parts of our cerebellum. Superstar Atlanta lawyer Don Keenan and his co-author David Ball have written about this primitive, or "reptilian," part of our brain. In the book they researched with insightful Wyoming trial lawyer Jim Fitzgerald, entitled *Reptile*,[1] they discuss the villainous conduct likely to make jurors concerned about their own safety and act to protect themselves and the community.

Identifying Villains

Identifying the villain in our clients' stories is difficult because they don't self-identify by wearing a shark fin, black plastic masks, or black capes.[2] Our antagonists often wear expensive suits and meet in tastefully appointed corporate boardrooms where decisions are driven by profit, not the safety of the people down on the street, far below the thirty-fifth floor. The evil they do is in secret, with a veneer of acceptable business practices. These villains are

1. Don Keenan and David Ball, *Reptile: The 2009 Manual of the Plaintiff's Revolution* (New York: Balloon Books, 2009).

2. Although the image of Sauron's giant, all-powerful, all-reaching evil eye is a wonderful analogy for certain corporations.

more like Gordon Gekko in the movie *Wall Street*, who espoused the mantra that "greed is good."

Don't be fooled by the suits. To find the villains, ask the following questions.

Who Was the Obvious Villain?

Who was the obvious beneficiary of the selfish actions, or decision not to act, in your case? The obvious beneficiary of misconduct is most easily identifiable in vehicle collision cases. In a car crash, the frontline villain is the person who obtains the small, momentary benefit of immediate gratification by texting while driving, speeding, or running a red light to save a bit of time. A person who chooses to break the law in one of those ways makes the decision to endanger everyone else on the roadway.

As the risk to others increases from the selfish choice, the villainy worsens. Take, for example, the off-duty police officer who activates his lights, but not his sirens, just so he can speed home through red lights at 2:00 a.m. and broadsides a car carrying two sisters, killing one and seriously injuring the other. There is the villain we think of every time we are sandwiched between two massive semitrucks on the freeway—the amphetamine-popping truck driver in his eighteenth hour driving without sleep, trying to move the freight as fast as he can to make more money.

On the Darth Vader end of the spectrum, the drunk driver has become the scourge, the demonized villain of the highways, all because of the basest of self-interest—the personal pleasures of intoxicating liquor. While drinking is legal for adults, the self-serving bad act comes from the choice to drive home (or to another bar) rather than endure the relatively minor inconvenience of taking a taxi, calling a sober friend for a ride, or having a designated driver. The ubiquity of cell phones has made the community-threatening decision to drive drunk inexcusable.

Who Was the Hidden Villain?

Was there a veiled or hidden villain—the true, but hidden beneficiary of the misconduct or systematic failure in the case? While visible villains are easy to identify, finding the veiled villain may take some work. Was there someone or some corporation up the chain from the bad actor who benefited from the system that was in place or made the decisions that created the bad situation?

Let's take a real-life case. SAE fraternity members at the University of New Mexico drugged an eighteen-year-old freshman girl with the date rape drug Rohypnol (roofies) at their annual "Cherry Bust" party. Once she was unconscious, the frat boys bent her over the tailgate of a truck and lined up to have sex with her limp body in the parking lot.

The visible villains in this case are obvious—the men who decided to drug and rape this innocent young girl. But what of the adults who supervised this fraternity house and, taking an even wider view, made the policies for SAE fraternities on a national basis?

Through discovery we learned that the national governing body of the SAEs, grown men extending the fond memories of their fraternity years, knew about similar incidents of rape at fraternity houses across the country, extending back for years. The recipe for rape was consistent. It was young men plus alcohol in an unsupervised frat house.

Approximately two years before the SAE fraternity members raped our client, the national governing body voted on whether to ban alcohol at all frat houses across the nation. On one side were those who were concerned about the rapes, deaths (falling off balconies or alcohol toxicity), and injuries from underage drinking (since most college SAEs were still under the age of twenty-one). On the other side were those who nostalgically believed that drinking and wild parties were what made fraternity life special and, if alcohol were banned, membership (and the dues from membership that supported the national organization) would drop. Based on what the fraternity members did to our client and what young fraternity members continue to do in fraternity houses across the country, you can guess how the vote went. It wasn't even close. The national organization put its own financial interests above safety. Which brings us to the third question you ask to find the villain in your case.

FOLLOW THE MONEY

One of the most effective ways of finding the true villain in your case is to follow the money. Who is making the most money or obtaining the most benefit from the misconduct?

The flow of money may come not from one big payoff, but in smaller amounts that the villain saves on a daily basis with a system designed to cut costs at the expense of safety. The longer the villain has had the system in place, the more risk there has been to all members of the community before your client ever walked in the door. Most often, because of the monetary benefit, that system will not have been fixed at the time of your lawsuit and is continuing to place others at risk.

We saw this kind of systemic failure when a national hospital chain came in and took over a hospital in Las Cruces, New Mexico.[3] The national corporation made the economic decision to spend money on advertising to fill its emergency room with patients. When those patients began flowing in, the corporation refused staff requests to increase the number of emergency room doctors and staff to handle the increased number of patients. Instead, to save more costs, it replaced many of the higher-paid ER doctors with lower-paid nurses, preferably male nurses. Wearing the same white coats and stethoscopes, they made most patients wrongly assume they had seen a doctor after a visit with the male nurse.

Of course, that paragraph of description took many more than one hundred hours of discovery to unearth. With the other

3. *Susan Weckesser, as Conservator of the Estate of Joseph Mendoza, an adult incapacitated person, Hector Mendoza and Stella Mendoza v. PHC-Las Cruces*, First Judicial District Court, case number D-101-CV-2010-00452.

side fighting discovery all the way, we had to get the court to order production of the advertising and marketing plans, the ads for increasing emergency room patients, the numbers that tracked the increased patients, the staff complaints, and requests for increased staffing contained in the minutes of medical meetings.

Into this overflowing, overtaxed, and understaffed emergency room walked a twenty-three-year-old young man with an imminently treatable, but potentially life-threatening, epiglottitis. Epiglottitis is an infection of the throat that can close a person's airway. If medical providers suspect epiglottitis, they should never leave the patient, they should have equipment nearby to re-establish the airway, and providers should never touch or aggravate the throat.

A male nurse saw our client, Joseph Mendoza, and Joseph and his family believed this male nurse was a doctor. Although the nurse suspected epiglottitis, the emergency room staff sent Joseph to wait for hours in the waiting room, where he had more and more difficulty breathing. After his mother went to the admission desk three times to request help, a staff member swabbed his throat (improperly touching the throat) and left him alone in an X-ray room. It was there that his throat closed completely and he had no oxygen for thirteen to fifteen minutes. This is the young man who never walked or spoke again because of the permanent anoxic brain injury that resulted from his mistreatment.

Although the obvious villains were the medical staff members who ignored Joseph, the true villains were those back in the corporate offices in Tennessee, who made a few extra dollars every day by luring patients to an emergency room that didn't have enough staff to provide quality care to those who responded to their advertising. In Elizabeth Garcia's case we identified the obvious villain, then we followed the money to find the hidden villains.

12

VILLAINS IN ELIZABETH GARCIA'S CASE

The obvious villain in Elizabeth Garcia's murder was the unknown man who kidnapped her, raped her, and stabbed her fifty-six times. Because there was no video camera in the Allsup's store, no one knew who he was. Police didn't catch methamphetamine user Paul Lovett until two years later, after he sexually assaulted and killed a second time, this time murdering a woman he knew. The police matched the DNA in that case to Elizabeth's killing. Lovett was ultimately convicted of first-degree murder in both killings and given a double life sentence.

Was there also a hidden villain in Elizabeth's murder?

On the surface, Lonnie and Barbara Allsup were an American success story. With a few years of college at Hardin-Simmons University in Abilene, Texas, for Lonnie, and a high school diploma for Barbara, the couple started a business called Lonnie's Drive-In Grocery in Roswell, New Mexico, in 1956. Over the years they built their company into the largest convenience store chain in the Southwest, with 310 stores in New Mexico, Texas, and Oklahoma. As they climbed the ladder of success, buying an oil company, a communications company, and a 2,300-acre ranch near Farwell, Texas, Lonnie Allsup had become the seventh richest man in the state by 1996, with Allsup's reporting annual revenues that year of $180 million.[1] The Allsup's corporation stayed a family-owned business, with all profits going solely to Lonnie and Barbara Allsup. As the Allsups acquired more and more, their employees on the front lines were left farther and farther behind, keeping the stores open twenty-four hours a day for minimum wage and no benefits.

Elizabeth Garcia was hired to work the graveyard shift for $5.25 an hour (ten cents more than minimum wage).[2] Out of her first couple of paltry paychecks, the company would have deducted the cost of the company uniform shirts she had been required to wear.[3] The only "free" benefit Allsup's clerks had was the state-mandated workers' compensation insurance, which paid them two-thirds of their minimum wage if they were injured so severely they could no longer work.

In the early 1990s, the Allsup's corporation filed a lawsuit against their workers' compensation carrier in an action known as the *North River* case. This lawsuit claimed that the insurance company had failed to adequately advise the Allsup's corporation on security measures for their stores, which would have helped them reduce injuries to their clerks and thus reduce the amount of workers' compensation benefits and premiums paid.[4]

Allsup's corporation presented an expert witness, Robert Epstein from Risktech Inc., who testified that if the workers' compensation insurance company had just informed Allsup's

---

1. About Allsup's, modified 2012, http://www.allsups.com/about; *McConnell v. Allsup's*, Lonnie Allsup deposition; *McConnell v. Allsup's*, Barbara Allsup deposition.

2. Partial Transcript of Proceedings, *McConnell v. Allsup's*, Barbara Allsup testimony, TR-66.

3. *Id.* at TR-66–67.

4. *Allsup's Convenience Stores, Inc. v. Crum and Forester Commercial Insurance and Its Joint Venture, Including North River Insurance Company and the United States First Insurance Company*, Second Judicial District Court, State of New Mexico, case number CV 90-07953.

of the security measures it should have been using in its stores to prevent crime, employee injuries could have been reduced by 64 percent. The security measures he said would have protected the clerks were closed-circuit surveillance cameras, bulletproof barricades between the employee and customers, armed security guards, and a written security training program for the employees. After a multi-week trial, the jury sided with Allsup's and awarded the company $17 million in damages, in part because of the insurance company's supposed failure to inform them about security devices for the store. The Allsups received their first payment of over $9.5 million from that lawsuit on November 14, 1994.[5]

We asked Lonnie Allsup in his deposition about whether he spent any of the *North River* settlement money for the security devices that had been recommended in that case and that had helped provide the basis for the damages Allsup's claimed against its insurance company:

Q: You didn't use any of the money from that lawsuit, or any other money Allsup's made during that time period, to install bulletproof barricades to protect your clerks from 1993 to 2002, when Ms. Garcia was killed?

A: No, I did not.

Q: There were no bulletproof enclosures installed by January 2002, were there, at any Allsup's store?

A: No, there was not.

Q: There was none installed at the Hobbs Allsup's store where Elizabeth Garcia was required to work alone on the graveyard shift, was there, sir?

A: No.[6]

---

5. Partial Transcript of Proceedings, *McConnell v. Allsup's*, Barbara Allsup testimony, April 2, 2008, TR-135.

6. *McConnell v. Allsup's*, Lonnie Allsup deposition, March 9, 2006, p. 108–109.

The first payment from the *North River* case came shortly after the state Environmental Improvement Board (EIB), the group charged with enforcing Occupational Safety and Health Administration (OSHA) regulations, cited Allsup's in 1994 for not having security in its Tucumcari store where a thirty-three-year-old mother of three was murdered on August 18, 1994, in her sixth week on the job. This woman was also named Elizabeth. Working alone on the graveyard shift, Elizabeth Williams was taken into the walk-in cooler and shot in the back of the head after she gave the robber the small amount of money kept in the cash register. The personal panic alarm Allsup's had given her had set off so many false alarms (for which the alarm company charged the store) that the store had discontinued using it.

After Ms. Williams's death, on January 12, 1995, the clerks at the Tucumcari store, Allsup's Store No. 58, sent an anonymous letter to the state Environmental Improvement Board[7], as well as a copy to Allsup's. The letter complained about the dangerous conditions in which the employees had to work. It reported that the only precaution Allsup's had implemented after Ms. Williams's murder had been to allow double coverage on the graveyard shift for three weeks. No security cameras, security guards, or any other safety measures were put into place, and the double coverage had been stopped because the store manager said the store didn't make enough money to justify a second clerk.

In the letter, the clerks wrote:

> Nothing has been done to change policy or make the stores safer since this incident . . . None of the Allsups have mentioned there (sic) regrets over the incident to anyone in the store to date. It seems to us that they are only concerned about the amount

---

7. Employees of Allsup's Store No. 58 to New Mexico Environmental Improvement Board, January 12, 1995, attached to Serious Violation issued to Allsup's on January 11, 1995, after the death of Elizabeth Williams. You can download a copy of this letter, called "Letter to New Mexico EIB," at http://www.trialguides.com/resources/downloads/changing-laws.

of money it has cost them or will cost them to date and not what it would cost to make the store safer.

The 1994 letter compared Allup's Store No. 58 to the Town and Country store in Tucumcari which, since the killing, began closing at midnight " . . . because they do not feel the sales they have at that time of night warrants the risk of human life." The letter pointed out that the Circle K store in Tucumcari had cameras and two people working, as did all the rest of the stores in town that stayed open twenty-four hours a day. The letter pointed out that the annual cost to add a second clerk was just $9,100 per year and then asked this question:

> We feel that is a very low cost to keep the employees safe and isn't a human life worth considerably more than that?[8]

Unbeknownst to the clerks of Allsup's Store No. 58, they sent their letter just a month and a half after Allsup's received its first $9.5 million payment on the *North River* judgment. The letter ended by asking that something be done to make the stores safer other than just keeping small amounts of money in the registers. The clerks suggested closing the store at midnight if the company was unwilling to invest more in security.

The 1994 OSHA citation for a serious violation in the death of Elizabeth Williams was the first ever issued against any company in the state of New Mexico for workplace violence. Rather than spend money to heighten the security in its stores, Allsup's used its political clout and personal connections with Republican Lieutenant Governor Walter Bradley to get the citation withdrawn. Nothing was done to improve security in Allsup's stores after the 1994 killing and the OSHA citation. The recommendations of its own security expert were still not implemented by 1999, when the *North River* appeal ended and Allsup's received

8. Employees of Allsup's Store No. 58 to New Mexico Environmental Improvement Board.

the balance of the $17 million it won against its workers' compensation carrier.

Why hadn't Allsup's adopted the security measures that other convenience stores use to successfully reduce crime? We believed we had found the answer by following the money. Because Allsup's was a privately owned corporation, every dollar Lonnie and Barbara Allsup saved on costs went right into their own pockets at the end of year: whether it was keeping wages low, deciding not to install security cameras, or refusing to add a second clerk on the graveyard shift. The most significant amount of money saved came with their refusal to schedule a second clerk.

> $6.50 per hour
> × 56 hours a week *(7 days of graveyard shifts)*
> × 52 weeks a year
> + Social Security of 7.51%
> ---
> = $20,349.49 *(per year, per store)*

Multiplied by all 310 stores, this meant Allsup's was saving $6.3 million per year by not adding a second clerk. Rather than protect their clerks, the Allsups decided to keep the money.

The Allsups' true personalities were further illuminated when we took the depositions of Lonnie Allsup, Barbara Allsup, and their son, temporary acting President Mark Allsup.

Under oath in his deposition, when asked whether he knew the number of people killed in his stores over the years, Lonnie Allsup answered, "I do not."[9] Through our own investigation, we found at least eleven, although there may have been more. How did the Allsup's corporation treat those that died in the line of duty? Here is what Mr. Allsup said:

---

9. *McConnell v. Allsup's*, Lonnie Allsup deposition, October 24, 2007, p. 281–282. Nor could Mr. Allsup tell us how many women had been raped or clerks victimized over the years. *Id.* For the most part, he could not remember their names, not that of Eva Pellissier, whose throat had been cut, or the exact name of Elizabeth Williams who died in the Tucumcari store. *Id.*, 271–272.

Lonnie Allsup

Q: Did Allsup's do anything for the families of the people killed in the store other than provide them work comp benefits or the other benefits required by law?

A: No.

Q: Is there a memorial at Allsup's corporate with the names of people who died in your service?

A: No . . .

Q: Is there any kind of scholarship fund that you've created for the children of those who have been killed in your service?

A: No.[10]

A few minutes into Lonnie Allsup's second deposition, when my partner Elicia Montoya asked an innocuous question about how clerks were trained, he suddenly stood up and, excusing himself, called a break in the questioning, saying, "Goddam, recess."[11]

After he stormed out of our conference room alone, his attorney, Chris Key, said, "Cowboys don't like to be sat down in deposition. We'll calm him down."

---

10. *McConnell v. Allsup's*, Lonnie Allsup deposition, March 9, 2006, p. 41–42.

11. *McConnell v. Allsup's*, Lonnie Allsup deposition, Vol. II, October 24, 2007, p. 237.

Barbara Allsup

Barbara Allsup came to her deposition wearing a huge diamond ring. Dry-eyed and unapologetic, she spent her time defending their decisions over the years not to implement any security measures in the stores, other than those designed to protect cash and merchandise.

Mark Allsup's deposition was the most enlightening of all. During the time Elizabeth Garcia came to work at Allsup's, Mark was the acting president—making decisions about the day-to-day business operations. Mark came to work for Allsup's in 1984, in part on the promise that if he worked hard, he would someday be able to purchase stock and have an ownership interest in the company. His deposition testimony is as follows:

Q: The company is owned 100 percent by Barbara and Lonnie, is that correct?

A: That's right.

Q: [W]hen was the first time you brought up with them your interest in having an ownership interest in the company if you were going to work there?

A: Well, actually, when I went to work for them that was discussed.

Q: And when was that?

A: On, 1984, maybe.

Q: And the idea was to train you up in the company and you were—you, as the only son, were going to take over the company or have some ownership interest in the company?

A: Essentially.

Q: Okay. And that's what you believed all the years you worked there.

A: Yes.

Q: When did it become an issue that you approached them and said, okay, I've been here for you know, over ten, over fifteen years; I'd like an ownership interest in the company? When did that first become an issue?

A: I'd say, oh, about five years before I left.

Q: And who did you approach about that?

A: Well, Lonnie. That's who I worked for.

Q: [I]s he the one that ran the company?

A: Yeah. Well, he ran aspects of it. Barbara ran the office, but, yeah, he was the final say in the company. That's right.

Q: And what did he say when you went to him five years before you left and said, I want an ownership interest in the company?

A: Well, he said, we'll work on it. And so we had that conversation numerous times over the [last] five years, that we'll eventually get something done. But it just never did happen.

Q: Okay. And you finally gave up after five years?

A: Yeah. I finally gave up on it.

Q: Did he ever say why he was not making good on the discussion with you about giving you an ownership interest in the company?

A: He just said he couldn't. He just said he—you know, it had
    been part of him, for his—as long as he could remember and
    he just couldn't do it.[12]

By the time we took his deposition, Mark was no longer with
Allsup's. He had quit in March 2002, after working for the company for fifteen years, waiting in vain for his father to keep his
promise to give him an ownership interest in the company.[13]

From these facts, the jury would have to decide who the villains were in our case and whether to award damages based, in
part, on the money Allsup's had saved by not installing security
devices for its employees. However, money wasn't the only justice
the Garcia family wanted.

---

12. *McConnell v. Allsup's*, Mark Allsup deposition, November 14, 2007, p. 13–15.

13. Partial transcript of Proceedings, *McConnell vs. Allsup's*, Barbara Allsup testimony, April 2, 2008, TR-109-110.

13

BEYOND THE MONEY

How I Came to Practice Transformative Law

S cratch the surface of public opinion on trial lawyers and here are the kinds of comments you get: "greedy," "selfish," and "all about the money."[1]

This view of trial lawyers even exists among members of the bar. Although most lawyers and law students deny that money is their primary motivation, they suspect that greed motivates other lawyers or law students. That misperception bleeds over onto our clients.

ARE CLIENTS REALLY LOOKING FOR MONEY?

Big business and the insurance industry encourage the public to misunderstand our clients. They'd like the public to think that

---

1. Interestingly, when asked about opinions of their own lawyers, the news is much better. The majority of people have a positive view of their own lawyers. See the ABA survey, "Public Perception of Lawyers," April, 2002, ABA Section of Litigation, Leo J. Shapiro & Associates.

our fellow citizens are waiting—hoping to be the victim of some form of negligence. Whether the victim in a car collision, medical malpractice, or injury from a badly designed product, as soon as a person is injured or a family member is killed, the first response in this industry-created fantasy is, "Oh, goody. I've hit the jackpot and can now sue for a lot of money."

A jury panel member once expressed this cynical view in its most naked, crass form during jury selection in one of our cases involving a fifteen-year-old boy's death. We asked whether any of the prospective panel would have any problems awarding monetary damages in the case. One man raised his hand and said, right in front of the grief-stricken parents who were sitting at the counsel table, "Well, I don't think parents should get lucky just because their kid was killed."

The truth is that, in cases where there is a serious injury or death, no one has ever come into my office and asked how much money the case is worth. In the depths of despair, some are angry, some are lost, and nearly all express the sentiment that they never thought they would be the kind of person to ever hire a lawyer. Having experienced the worst thing in their lives, they want you to find the reason the unthinkable has happened and find a way to prevent it from happening to anyone else.

The Check She Wouldn't Collect

I learned this lesson early in my career in the case of a woman whose oldest son, while riding his motorcycle, had been killed by a drunk driver. The drunk driver had the minimum state-required liability coverage of $25,000, which his insurance company quickly tendered and paid. When a case settles, most clients can't wait to pick up their settlement proceeds.

Once the settlement check arrived at our office, the boy's mother would not come pick it up. We called her. She did not come. We sent letters. She did not come. We sent certified letters. She still did not come. Two months after the check arrived, I left a message telling her I would have to come to her house if she did not come meet me at my office at a specified time.

On the day of the appointment, she arrived late, dragging herself into the office as if she believed something horrible was about to happen. As I had her read the release and explained it, I was unsure if she was really hearing me. She numbly signed the document, and then I set the check down on the desk between us.

She did not pick it up. When I pushed the check toward her, she drew back and suddenly burst into tears. "I don't want it," she said through her sobs, then articulated the source of her distress and her irresolvable dilemma: "How can I take money for my son's death?"

This is how I learned early in my career that when someone's child is killed, the case is never about the money. For this poor mother, we talked about what she could do with this money to honor her son or to make a difference in the world. After an hour of discussing what her son had been like and what he would have wanted, she decided to donate the entire amount to Mothers Against Drunk Driving.

PRACTICING TRANSFORMATIVE LAW

That case made me rethink the way I was practicing law. In each case, I began asking what could be done to make a difference, to prevent the wrongdoing that caused the death or injury, and to help—really help—our clients.

This transformation started by asking our clients to come up with a list of things they would like the defendant to do, separate from a monetary award. In addition to the many changes in safety policies and procedures that our clients have suggested over the years, one of the most common requests on the list is for a written apology from the wrongdoer.

This simple request for accountability, for acceptance of responsibility, is instructive on the public's view of what true justice looks like. In addition to making sure there is enough money to take care of an injured person, a jury trial is an attempt to force public accountability on a company or person who has refused to apologize or accept fault.

New Approaches to Settlement

We have two basic approaches to practicing what our firm has come to call *transformative law*. The first is to present the other side with a wish list, a list of changes you would like to see the company make, and let them know you will not present them with a settlement number or attend a mediation until you have agreed on the changes they will make to prevent their wrongdoing from happening again.

The second approach is my favorite. Instead of a drop-dead demand for change, you tell the defendant you will start settlement negotiations at $5 million if they make no changes. But if they make the following changes, you will start settlement negotiations at $2 million. This kind of offer immediately lets you know what kind of defendant you are dealing with.

In truth, if this was a decent or "good" company that cared about its employees or customers, it would have made the safety changes to prevent harm immediately after someone was hurt or killed and *before* you filed a lawsuit. It should not have required filing a lawsuit to make safety changes take place. Unfortunately, that rarely happens. By the time we file suit, sometimes a year or two after the injury or death, companies have often done nothing to correct the problem, exposing further patients, consumers, or the general public to the continued risk of danger.

Over time, we have only had about 40 percent of defendants agree to make changes and start at the lower number. For the approximately 60 percent of the defendants who decide to make no changes and start negotiations at the higher number, the response is usually something like this:

> If we make these safety changes, our company will
> have to pay for them and reduce our bottom line.

If you get a big verdict or settlement, our insurance company will have to pay for it. So, we're starting at the higher number.

What does that tell you about the defendant, whether an individual or a corporation?

This behavior is morally bankrupt, and you should have no qualms in proceeding full bore ahead to let a jury put the wood to them at trial.

A Suicide and a Police Department

One of the first times we used this approach was in the case of Larry Harper.[2] Larry was a young man who had a suffered a series of temporary personal setbacks and decided to go up into the mountains outside of Albuquerque to kill himself. Before heading up the unpopulated mountain, he called his brother to say goodbye and to pass on a final message to his wife, Hope.

His brother James first called the Albuquerque Suicide Prevention Hotline. No one answered. He then called the Albuquerque Police Department (APD), who told him and the rest of Larry's family to meet them at the bottom of the mountain where Larry had walked up the hill.

Larry Harper

2. *Hope Harper v. The City of Albuquerque*, United States District Court, District of New Mexico, case number CIV 96-1048 BB/WWD.

The family was not aware that the APD was notorious for shooting and killing more citizens per capita than any other police department in the country (a dark distinction that, unfortunately, continues to this day), including many people who were threatening suicide. Despite being unaware of the APD's history, the assembled family members quickly became disturbed when, instead of a team of psychologists, the APD sent out their SWAT van. As one heavily armed tactical officer after another climbed out of the van and began loudly gearing up and clicking rounds into their shotguns, the family had a change of heart.

"Wait a minute," said Larry's brother and Larry's wife. "What are you guys doing? He's not a danger to anyone else; he's just depressed."

"Don't worry," the SWAT officers responded. "These guns are just loaded with nonlethal rounds."

That statement was a lie.

It was dark by the time the SWAT team was fully assembled, armed, and geared up. It was October, with the temperature dropped down near the thirties. Larry Harper had now been in the mountains for about two hours and did not have a coat.

The SWAT team could have just waited at the bottom of the hill and done any of the following:

- Waited until Larry Harper changed his mind and, after getting cold, came back to the lot where he had parked his truck.

- Sent the police psychologist up with an officer to try to talk to him.

- Waited until morning when it was light and gone up to see if there was a body to collect.

Any of these choices would have been preferable to the decision the police officers made next.

The APD SWAT team had just obtained some new night-vision goggles and, apparently, wanted the chance to try them out. Over the family's continued protests, they organized a military-style assault on the mountain, with nine officers and two police dogs sneaking up the hillside in the darkness for the next forty-five minutes.

And what of Larry Harper? He knew nothing about the police assault. After sitting in the cold night for two hours and forty-five minutes near the mountain spot where he and his wife had been married, we can only guess that he remembered the best thing about his life—his wife, Hope—and decided to come down the mountain and live.

With his gun put away in his waistband, he was walking down the middle of the dark road when, suddenly and without warning, he was lit up from three sides by men in black tactical uniforms and camouflage, pointing rifles at him, cursing and shouting for him to "drop the gun."

Without taking his gun out of his waistband, Larry Harper raised his hands and, perhaps having heard about the history of APD shooting unarmed people, asked a simple question.

"Will you put your guns down if I put my gun down?"

The answer, amid lots more shouting and cursing, was "No."

For the next several minutes there was a standoff, during which Larry Harper never touched or took out his weapon. When it became apparent the police were not going to back down, Larry Harper ran off the roadway, away into the darkness, yelling over his shoulder, "I'm not doing anything wrong. Just leave me alone."

The APD officers and dogs gave chase, up and down arroyos, poked by spiny yuccas in the dark, stomping into cactus plants, for more than thirty minutes. As they ran after Larry Harper in the dark, the two K-9 officers repeatedly asked for permission to unleash their dogs and let the animals take down Mr. Harper without using deadly force to stop him. The SWAT officer in charge refused their requests.

When Larry finally climbed into a tree, keeping the trunk between him and the officers he feared, the SWAT team ordered its sniper to take up a silent position off to his left. Without being able to see whether or not there was any threat, the SWAT sniper shot Mr. Harper out of the tree.

Out of the moonless darkness, Larry cried out in pain and shouted in surprise, "You shot me. I can't believe you shot me. I wasn't doing anything. My God, it hurts so bad."

Larry Harper was the one nonpolice witness to this shooting and he was still alive.

The SWAT sniper called for the other officers to "light him up." When they trained their flashlights back on him, he was doubled over a branch and still crying out in pain. The sniper shot him again, silencing him forever.[3]

When the sun came up, Larry Harper was dead. Up in the mountains, near where his body lay, the APD officers were all photographed in full gear (except for the sniper, whose gun was taken into evidence). The photos bore an eerie similarity to the kind of photos hunters take of their kill. The only thing missing was the body of Larry Harper strung up between two poles.

When we asked the officers in deposition why they had sent officers in tactical gear to deal with someone who had only

*A "trophy" photo blown up to life size to show how "comforting"
these officers would have appeared to Mr. Harper*

3. *Hope Harper v. The City of Albuquerque.* This is based on police reports and the officers' depositions.

threatened himself, the astounding answer was that they dressed that way because it "comforted" the suicidal citizen.

What did Larry Harper's family want? Obviously, they wanted Larry back, alive.

Since the sniper's two bullets made that wish impossible, they wanted to stop this from happening to anyone else. The family agreed to take less money even than the small, capped amount of damages they were entitled to, if APD would change some of its policies and practices to prevent this from ever happening again.

As a result of the family's decision to take less money for change, among other things, the APD agreed to do the following:

- Create a Crisis Intervention Team made up of officers specially trained to deal with suicidal citizens and those suffering from mental illness.

- Tape-record all future encounters with suicidal citizens (something they had not done with Mr. Harper).

- Promptly notify the family of the death of their loved one (although they were at the bottom of the hill, Larry's family was not told of his death until midday).

- Have the police psychologist offer the family counseling. In this case, the only person offered counseling was the police officer who shot Mr. Harper.

- Report back to the family on implementation of all these changes in one year.

Since the Harper case, other clients have asked for and gotten warning labels on unsafe products, changes in safety policies and procedures, and the retraining of hospital employees on the missed medical issues that caused injury to their patients. Some clients have even received an apology.

In many cases, these changes have meant more to our clients than the money they received to fix what was broken or to make up for what couldn't be fixed. While the money took care of their injured loved one, the changes meant no one else would have to suffer the death or catastrophic injury they experienced. The same was true for the family of Elizabeth Garcia.

There was not a sum of money large enough to fix the black hole caused by her death. Money could help Victorina Garcia raise Elizabeth's children. It could fill the children's lives with dance lessons, sports training, travel, and provide for their college educations—but it could not give Elizabeth back to her family, even for one day. Would the threat of a large verdict do what Allsup's had not done in the years since Elizabeth's death—cause Allsup's to change the unsafe security practices that still endangered the clerks and customers in its stores?

14

WOULD ALLSUP'S MAKE A CHANGE?

About a year into the case, when the lawyers for the convenience store were stonewalling us on producing internal crime reports, and we were still struggling to track down all of the crime statistics for each store on our own, we made a settlement offer to the Allsup's corporation. If the convenience store chain would agree to never again have clerks work alone on the graveyard shift, the family would accept only $3 million to settle the case.

Why did we offer to settle for such a small amount early in the case? Remember that the grandmother, Victorina, was now raising Elizabeth's three children on her own, and there were still three years of litigation before we would get to trial. At that point, we hadn't found all of the other crimes against Allsup's employees that would prove the reckless corporate conduct we needed to sue an employer outside of the New Mexico Workers' Compensation Act. Most importantly, the Garcia family wanted something to change so no other mothers, daughters, and fathers would be raped or killed while working alone on the graveyard shift without security.

What was Allsup's response to this extraordinarily generous settlement offer by the Garcia family?

Allsup's and their insurance company (a subsidiary of AIG) gave no response at all. They would not offer to pay anything to the family of the woman who died working for minimum wage as a human shield to protect their money and merchandise.

The family's reaction to Allsup's failure to respond to our initial settlement offer was to ask whether we could find some way to make change happen outside the courtroom or the legal system. That opportunity for change came in the form of the New Mexico Environmental Improvement Board. (Democratic Governor Bill Richardson, a strong proponent of worker safety, appointed the members of this board.)

After Elizabeth's death, the EIB sought funding from the state legislature to finance a study on convenience store crime across the state, looking at crimes in six communities from 1998 to April of 2002. Over those five years, the study found sixteen killings, twenty-four rapes, thirty-seven abductions, and thousands of other crimes at New Mexico convenience stores. Once the study was completed, the EIB, under chairwoman Gay Dillingham, held a series of hearings in different locations around the state on whether the state should enact regulations to protect convenience store workers.

The convenience store industry and the New Mexico Petroleum Marketers Association marshaled its army of paid lobbyists to oppose any regulations. Their argument was that no matter the kinds of dangers the convenience store owners chose to inflict upon their workers, the government should not be allowed to interfere with the free enterprise system. They objected to every proposal. Criminals were impossible to stop or deter, argued the convenience store lobbyists. They said video cameras had little or no deterrent effect, security guards were too expensive, and bullet-resistant enclosures scared customers away by revealing the truth—these were dangerous places at night. They paid to fly in their industry expert, Dr. Rosemary Erickson, to testify about her industry-funded studies and to oppose the regulation they feared the most—the one that would require two clerks to be on duty after dark. Although proven to be the most effective deterrent to crime in the Gainesville, Florida, study, the two-clerk regulation was the option that would cost the industry about $20,000 per year, per store—the cost of adding a second clerk.[1]

In response to this organized onslaught against the proposed regulations, all we had were the people who worked in the stores. Minimum-wage convenience store workers cannot afford lobbyists. They cannot hire expert witnesses to conduct studies. They do not have a union. Most are struggling day to day just to feed their families and make ends meet. In this fight against the convenience store industry and petroleum interests, what chance would they have?

As Margaret Mead famously said, "Never doubt that a small group of thoughtful, committed citizens can change the world; indeed, it's the only thing that ever has."[2]

So we began looking for people who would be willing to take time away from their jobs, travel to Santa Fe or other hearing locations around the state on their own dime, and stand up for the right of convenience store workers to be safe behind their cash registers. The response was extraordinary.

The family of Paul Sedillo came to testify how, after Circle K encouraged Paul to chase after shoplifters and people who drove off without paying for gas, Paul ran after some young men who

Paul Sedillo, Tracey Eldridge, and Amelia Sedillo

1. The math for calculating this number is in chapter 12, "Villains in Elizabeth Garcia's Case."

2. Margaret Mead may not have actually said this, but I like the quote anyway.

were trying to pass off a stolen credit card. He was shot in the heart, ran back into the store, and called 911 before he collapsed and died. Left alone as a result of Paul's death were his girlfriend, Tracey Eldridge, and his one-year-old daughter, Amelia.[3]

Ken Rummel

The family of Kenneth Rummel, a former client, offered testimony about how their father was working alone on the graveyard shift when he followed a company policy that required him to confront shoplifters. He asked the three young men in the store to put back a frozen pizza one of them had placed inside his jacket. When they refused, he went into an enclosed back room to call the police on the only phone in the store. The three men followed him into the room our security expert later called an inescapable "kill zone." They pulled the phone out of the wall and began beating Ken with it. When he fell to the floor, they kicked him over and over again in the face, fracturing the bones around his eye and forcing the shards into the frontal lobe of his brain.

As a result of his injuries, Ken lost his short-term memory and his ability to sequence his activities. Not only was he unable to work, his family had to closely watch him to make sure he didn't get lost or hurt. In one dramatic example, Ken's son, Ken Junior, talked about how he once took his dad to a job site where Junior was renovating a house. His dad disappeared, and after a frantic search for about an hour, they found him on the roof of the house,

---

3. *Eldridge v. Circle K Corp.*, 123 N.M. 145, 934 P.2d 1074 (Ct.App. 1997), *cert. den.* 1997.

walking in circles. His dad had seen a ladder and climbed up on the roof. Once up there, he couldn't remember how he had gotten there, and because his brain could no longer sequence the steps needed to complete a task, he couldn't figure out how to get down.

After a 1992 jury verdict against Circle K for $11.7 million ($1 million in compensatory damages and $10.7 million in punitive damages) and an appeal that lasted five years, Ken Rummel's family finally received the jury award ten years after Ken was injured. This was enough money to take care of him for the rest of his life, and Circle K began making the kinds of changes to its safety policies that the New Mexico EIB was now considering for all convenience stores.[4]

David Roemer, a former prison guard, testified that he was more fearful working alone on the graveyard shift in a convenience store than he had ever been in any prison he had ever worked. Not only did he feel that the crime rate was higher in convenience stores than in prisons, there also was no backup or security for the lone convenience store worker. When David asked whether he could bring a gun to work for protection, he was told "no." The store owner was concerned that if David shot someone who was trying to rob the store, the company could be sued.

To rebut the research by the industry-funded expert, Dr. Rosemary Erickson, we called Dr. Richard Swanson and let him know about the hearings on the proposed regulations. He came to the hearing on his own dime, unpaid by anyone. He testified about the results of his Gainesville study, which conclusively established the effectiveness of having two clerks present to reduce crime in convenience stores.

Anchoring all of these witnesses was the heart-wrenching testimony by Elizabeth Garcia's younger sister, Cecelia Garcia. With her long dark hair and the same sparkling eyes as her sister Elizabeth, she helped the Environmental Improvement Board understand the devastation that had been inflicted on her family as a result of Elizabeth's death. The echo of her sister's face in

---

4. *Rummel v. Lexington Ins. Co.,* 123 N.M. 752, 945 P.2d 970 (Ct. App. 1997), *cert. den.* 1997.

Cecelia's own features brought Elizabeth back to life in the hot, stale hearing room.

In hearing after hearing, these ordinary people and the members of our law firm showed up on their own time to make the case for regulating an industry that refused to regulate itself. It refused to spend money to make its workers safer.

Our presence was so ubiquitous, that at the third hearing, one of the industry's many paid lobbyists—a man wearing a sport coat, cowboy boots, and a diamond pinkie ring—approached me.

"I just want to know one thing," said the lobbyist. "Who's paying you to support these regulations?"

"No one," I answered.

"That's a bunch of bull," he said and then added some insight into his own personality. "No one does something for nothing."

I laughed. "Sorry to disappoint you, but we're just here because it's the right thing to do."

"I just don't believe you," he blustered before hustling back to the scrum of lobbyists, throwing one final parting shot over his shoulder, "I'll figure out who is sponsoring you. No one does anything for free."

He was wrong. Everyone who came for our side did so for free. The free testimony of the real-world workers won out over the moneyed interests of the New Mexico Petroleum Marketers Association and the convenience store industry. On June 1, 2004, the state of New Mexico enacted the strictest regulations in the country for convenience stores.

For the graveyard shift, from 11:00 p.m. to 7:00 a.m., all stores were now required to choose at least one security measure from the following list:

◆ Staff with two clerks.

◆ Staff with a clerk and a security guard.

◆ Place a lone clerk in a bullet-resistant enclosure.

◆ Close the store during those hours.

In addition, at all times of the day and night, convenience stores were required to install security cameras—the very thing Ms. Deibler had requested of Mark Allsup after the death of her husband in its Ruidoso store.

As a result of these regulations, no convenience store clerk was killed on the graveyard shift in New Mexico for eight years. Following implementation of the regulations, a state Environment Department study of convenience store crimes in six communities found assaults and robberies were down by an annual average of about 92 percent and theft and larcenies dropped 88 percent.[5]

The Allsups' response to the regulations? I asked Barbara Allsup about that when she was on the witness stand:

Q: In June of 2004, the New Mexico OSHA passed a whole set of regulations that related specifically to convenience stores, did they not?

A: Yes, they did.

Q: And you were not in favor of those regulations, were you, Mrs. Allsup?

A: No, ma'am.[6]

In the years between implementation of the regulations and our jury trial, Allsup's took several steps to overturn the regulations because, as Lonnie Allsup revealed in his deposition:

A: We don't feel the government should interfere in business to that extent and we don't agree with all of the rules that they placed in.

Q: Which ones don't you agree with?

5. "New Mexico Convenience Store Crime Drops after 2004 Rules," *Claims Journal*, September 3, 2008, http://www.claimsjournal.com/news/west/2008/09/03/93315.htm.

6. Partial Transcript of Proceedings, *McConnell v. Allsup's*, April 2, 2008, p. 54.

A: We don't agree with the two clerks.[7]

Allsup's hired a lawyer to file an appeal of the regulations. The company also made over $82,000 in political contributions (enough to add a second clerk on the graveyard shift in four different stores for a whole year), including a contribution to the New Mexico Petroleum Marketers Association to try to get the regulations overturned in the legislature.[8] A bill was floated in the New Mexico legislature to undo the regulations the year after they went into effect.

This meant marshaling the ordinary citizens once again to travel to Santa Fe to fight this effort by testifying in committee hearings. Our office put together a briefing book for each of the legislators containing the stories of all those whose lives had been affected by convenience store crime. This time, we enlisted the power of the media to let the public know how the industry was trying to undo these safety regulations. After a television reporter with a camera chased around the legislator who had sponsored the bill and who kept ducking out of conferences and sneaking out of his office to avoid the cameras, the bill was quietly killed in committee.

The ordinary citizens won again. The appeal did not overturn the EIB regulations. Those regulations are still law in the state of New Mexico and are still protecting convenience store workers on the graveyard shift.

With the help of the Garcia family and other workers, we had defeated the industry-funded expert witness and her biased studies. But it wouldn't prevent Allsup's from trying to defeat us at trial with other highly paid expert witnesses.

7. Lonnie Allsup deposition, Vol. II, October 24, 2007, p. 266.

8. Lonnie Allsup deposition, p. 55–56.

15

CROSS-EXAMINING THE
BEST EXPERTS MONEY CAN BUY

One of the problems with deciding to make a career out of representing David (or his wife) against Goliath is that Goliath always has more resources. Nowhere is this more apparent than in the area of expert witnesses.

When you are taking on a business, you will often find that the expert witnesses you need have already been co-opted by industry. Whether you are involved in a products liability case, a toxic exposure case, or a medical malpractice case, it is not unusual to find that the other side controls 90 percent of the scientists or expert witnesses you might want to take a look at your case. How does this happen?

Industry funds the studies and research of scientists, academicians, and medical schools. Unfortunately, he who pays the piper also calls the tune. Although it is never in writing, even the most ethical researcher understands that if the $2 million annual study grant given to his or her institution results in a finding that the donor company's product is toxic to humans or unreasonably dangerous, that researcher will not be getting funding from said company the following year.

Massive amounts of money result not only in studies that support industry positions, but also in a stable of expert witnesses willing to step forward and defend industry practices. While a plaintiffs' lawyer may hire a particular kind of expert only once or twice in her career, businesses and industry groups may be involved in repeated lawsuits across the country. A scientist or researcher who testifies for the defense will have years of work ahead. Those who testify for a lone plaintiff can never be guaranteed they will ever testify again.

Defeating a Defense Expert with a Grapefruit

A prime example is the California medical doctor who came up with a defense theory that reaped him a fortune in fees for his expert testimony. His theory was that once a cancerous tumor was large enough to be detected by an X-ray, it was too late to save the patient because it had already metastasized (the process of shedding cancerous cells that migrate to other organs).

As you might expect, this made him the go-to doctor in every cancer misdiagnosis case around the country. Even though a patient's tumor was clearly visible on an X-ray or scan and was something the doctor should have caught and treated, this expert witness would come in to testify, "So what? Based on my theory, the patient was already dead anyway."

This testimony had made him very rich. He pulled in over $1 million a year as an expert witness. The problem came with how he made the rest of his money. He made another half million a year as a practicing oncologist, one who would treat cancer patients whose tumors *had* been detected on X-rays. As he ordered expensive treatment after expensive treatment for his patients, he never told them what he went around the country telling juries—his belief that once their tumor was large enough to show up on an X-ray, all treatment was futile because it was too late and they were going to die.

When I asked him why he didn't share his theory with the cancer patients he was treating, he smiled and said, "Well, people need to have hope." Because of his patients' hope, he kept billing for the same treatment that he regularly testified was completely unnecessary.

Jurors hate hypocrisy. After cross-examining him on this irresolvable conflict, that is, that either his theory was bogus or he was taking advantage of cancer patients by billing them for treatment they didn't need, I made him into a trial exhibit.

I asked the distinguished-looking defense doctor with silver hair like Lee Iacocca to step down from the witness stand in his expensive bespoke suit. From a brown paper bag, I took out a yellow object.[1]

Q: Doctor, can you please tell me what this is?

A: Why, yes. That's a California grapefruit.

Q: That is correct, doctor. Now, if you can just stand here in front of the jury and hold that grapefruit up in the spot right where it was found on Victoria Dudley's X-ray, I'd like to try to understand this theory you've testified about.

A: Okay.

[The doctor held the grapefruit up to his chest.]

Q: Now as I understand metastasis, it is when cells break off the cancerous tumor and begin floating around in the body, is that correct?

[I took out a stack of yellow sticky notes.]

A: Yes.

[The doctor still held the grapefruit.]

Q: Some of these floating cancerous cells are killed off by the body's immune system, and die?

---

1. The following testimony is from my trial notes, not verbatim.

[I pulled some of the sticky notes off the grapefruit and threw them into the air where they fell to the floor.]

A: Yes.

[The doctor still held the grapefruit.]

Q: And if you can cut out the tumor at that point, a person will survive their cancer, won't they?

A: Yes.

[The doctor was still holding the grapefruit.]

Q: But your testimony is that, once a tumor is big enough to see on an X-ray, the cancer has already migrated somewhere else, perhaps to the next closest group of lymph nodes, which would be somewhere here in the middle of your tie, is that right?

A: Yes.

[Said the doctor holding a grapefruit.]

Q: *[And then, in my sweetest voice, I asked him,]* Can I put these sticky notes on you?

[It was an interesting choice for him. He could say no to my simple request and look like a bad sport, or he could say yes.]

A: Yes.

[Said the doctor holding a grapefruit.]

So I stuck sticky notes in the middle of his tie, and then at the next group of lymph nodes at the top of his tie, and then on the shirt at the base of his neck. As the sticky notes went on, the jury began to giggle, stifled at first, but as more and more sticky notes were stuck onto the grapefruit-holding doctor, the laughter grew louder. Even the previously stoic woman judge, Susan Conway, had her face buried behind a file folder that appeared to be shaking.

By the end of my series of questions, the doctor was so flustered by the laughing jury that when I released him to go back to the stand, he took the grapefruit with him. It wasn't until halfway through the re-direct by the defense lawyer that he realized he was still covered with sticky notes and began snatching them off his jacket and tie.

The jury rejected the defense expert's testimony and found that the defendant doctor was negligent for not spotting on her X-ray the lung tumor that ultimately killed my forty-year-old client and misdiagnosing her yearlong cough and chest pain as mycoplasma pneumonia. The visual image of the expert holding a grapefruit while covered in sticky notes was all the jury could remember of the man, and it totally destroyed whatever credibility he had left after they'd learned about the hypocritical way in which he made money.

Because this was such an unusual and unexpected approach to cross-examination, the defense lawyers never made a single objection, but sat back and watched, open-mouthed. There really isn't a rule of evidence that prohibits you from making a defense witness into a demonstrative aid, particularly if the expert consents in advance.

Of course, you can't "grapefruit" most experts. You can only use such a heavy-handed cross-examination technique on someone whom you have already proven to the jury is worthy of ridicule or disdain. You have to be able to see the witness through the juror's eyes. If the jury is not there with you yet, attempting this kind of thing too early or with the wrong witness will make you seem like you are being unfair to the witness. With the right discredited witness, it is heaven.

It's those kinds of cross-examination moments in the courtroom that trial lawyers live for. As my husband (a samurai trial lawyer in his own right before he took a government job) is fond of saying, "A good cross-examination is the most fun a trial lawyer can have with his clothes on." Hmmm, I hope this is not really a comment on our sex life.

FINDING WHAT YOU NEED
FOR CROSS-EXAMINATION

What approaches, other than the grapefruit, can you use on your expert witness?

A good cross of an expert begins with the same kind of extensive research into the person you should do for everything and everyone in the case (one hundred hours for every hour in the courtroom). You should do this research not the day before cross-examination, but before the expert's deposition. Here's where you look:

1. Google the expert.

   » Find the description of their title, the services they provide, and where they work. Does what they do for a living contradict or complement their role as an expert?

   » Do they have a website advertising their services as an expert? If so, read through the whole thing, every page. There you may find gems like this slogan: "The Voice of the Defense."

   » Have they written articles or letters to the editor with a particular slant?

   » Are they a member of an expert-for-hire service? How does that service advertise what it does?

   » Are they on Facebook or do they post or blog on other social media sites?

2. Research the expert on listservs.

   Get on every listserv that you can and see if anyone else knows or has experience with this expert. If you don't belong to a lawyer listserv, you are missing out on the greatest resource since the invention of the Internet.

3. Track down the expert's past testimony.

Once you get a list of the expert's past testimony, try to track down every deposition or trial transcript you can get your hands on (listserv buddies may help reduce the work needed for this task). The most important depositions and transcripts to obtain are those rare occasions where the expert has testified on the side of the case you are representing.

4. Run a case search on the expert.

Run the expert's name through your legal research database to see if they appear in any appellate opinions, either allowing their testimony or, more important for you, excluding their testimony.

5. Consult other experts.

Some of the most valuable cross-examination material I've ever received against an expert has come from my own expert witness in the same field.

QUESTIONING A POLYGRAPH EXPERT

Before the Internet, it was from my own expert, world-renowned polygrapher David Raskin, that I learned about the eccentric research done by defense polygrapher and early polygraph pioneer Cleve Backster, who passed away in 2013. Unbeknownst to the defense lawyer who hired him, Mr. Backster believed that non-human subjects could be polygraphed and, late at night, alone in his lab, had done a series of experiments to prove that theory.[2] The following is an approximation of my cross-examination about those experiments:

Q: Now, Mr. Backster, in addition to your research in the early days of the polygraph, you have performed a series of

2. This cross-examination is from trial notes and my memory.

experiments trying to prove that the reactions of nonhuman subjects can be measured by the polygraph, is that right?

A: Why, yes.

[He sat up a little prouder on the witness stand while, at the defense table, the lawyers perked up at this unknown information.]

Q: In one experiment, you took one egg out of a carton and hooked it up to the polygraph. Then, you took one of its fellow eggs out of the carton and, in front of the other egg, dropped the second egg into boiling water. Is that right?

A: Yes.

Q: And it was your conclusion from that experiment that the polygraph registered a reaction from the egg connected to the machine, is that right?

A: Yes.

[The defense lawyers sank a little lower in their seats.]

Q: You did a similar experiment with yogurt from the same container?

A: Yes.

Q: In which you hooked up a dollop of yogurt and destroyed the rest of the yogurt culture in its presence?

A: Yes.

Q: And it was your conclusion from that experiment that the surviving yogurt organisms reacted badly to their friends being killed?

A: Yes.

[The defense lawyers began looking down and shuffling papers.]

Q: Because of this theory, when a local police department called you in to polygraph a large number of suspects in a murder case, you had a better idea. Instead of polygraphing the many human suspects, you suggested to the department that they let you polygraph the two houseplants that had been in the room when the murder occurred, isn't that right?

A: Yes.

Q: What you did was to hook up the two plants to a polygraph and then walk all the suspects by the plants to see which one they reacted to?

A: Yes.

Q: Did those plants come and testify at trial?

Q: No.

[He sadly shook his head.]

Q: They couldn't identify the murderer.

Although the defense lawyers looked miserable as I destroyed their expert's credibility, Mr. Backster was outwardly unaffected by his cross-examination. His parting comment from the stand was, "You know, they laughed at Galileo too." Today, you can Google him and find this still-unaccepted research online, waiting for the rest of the world to catch up with him.

APPROACHES TO CROSS-EXAMINING EXPERT WITNESSES

After finding all you can about opposing experts, never forget that they will always know more than you about their own area of expertise. If you try to take on the expert on his or her own field, you will get massacred. When I am cross-examining an expert, I like to imagine that she is holding a small cannon, just waiting for me to give her an opening to blast me. This image focuses your attention to help you make sure all your leading questions are tight and you have your control techniques at the ready.

You need to decide on your approach and theme with each expert, remembering that the harsher the position you take, the more evidence you need to back it up. From lesser extreme to harsher extreme, here are three examples to help you identify how best to cross-examine expert witnesses:

1. The expert is wrong because the other side has not provided her all the information she needs to make a correct decision in the case.

   ◆ *Theme: Junk In, Junk Out*

2. The expert is biased in favor of one side:

   » Because she only reviews cases or testifies for that side.

   » Because she makes a living, researches, or works on only one side, or is defending the profession.

   » Because she is being paid huge amounts of money.

   ◆ *Theme(s): Follow the Money, Self-Interest, He Who Pays the Piper Calls the Tune*

3. The expert is lying for the money.

   ◆ *Theme: Actions Speak Louder than Words*

You can build a good cross-examination around any of these themes and theories—or one you come up with on your own. Start by headlining your theme so the jury knows your view of this expert from the start.

Use the Expert's Own Procedures

For example, in our earlier lack of security case against a Circle K convenience store, in which three men beat up a lone late-night clerk, we learned that the defense's security expert owned a security company. After obtaining the policies and procedures from his company in discovery, we put together a cross-examination that went something like this:[3]

Q: You have heard the phrase, "Actions speak louder than words"?

A: Yes.

Q: What that means is that, if you really want to know what someone believes, you should look at what they do rather than what they say?

A: I guess that's right.

Q: Now, in this case, you have testified that it was perfectly all right for the convenience store to make its clerks work alone, is that right?

A: Yes, that was my testimony.

Q: In addition to being an expert witness, you run a security company, do you not?

A: That's correct.

Q: You have written policies and procedures for the people you hire as security guards?

A: Yes.

Q: And one of your written policies requires that your security guards work in teams, isn't that correct?

A: Yes.

Q: Because, as you say in your manual, "There Is Safety in Numbers."

A: That's what it says.

Q: In fact, for that reason, your own employees are never allowed to work without a second security officer?

A: Yes.

---

3. This cross-examination is not exact, but comes from my trial notes.

Q: Almost all of the security guards you hire are ex–law enforcement officers, isn't that right?

A: Yes.

Q: People who have had training in dealing with dangerous criminals?

A: Yes.

Q: Who have had more extensive training than the minimum-wage clerks who work in convenience stores?

A: I guess so.

Q: And yet, the rule in your business for your trained ex–police officers is that they never approach anyone without a second person?

A: That is correct.

Q: For the people you hire as security guards, you think it is important that they have training in how to deal with potentially dangerous people?

A: Yes.

Q: Even though you've testified here that it was okay for the convenience store not to provide any training for its clerks?

A: Yes.

Q: Now, you've also said it was okay for the convenience store to require its untrained clerks to approach suspicious persons in the store, is that right?

A: That was my testimony.

Q: In your business, your rule for your security guards is that, if they see a suspicious person, they are not supposed to approach the person, but are supposed to call law enforcement to respond?

A: Yes.

Q: Even though most of the guards are ex–law enforcement themselves, that is your policy?

A: Yes . . . for their safety.

Q: That is exactly right.

As we went through the questions, I created a handwritten chart as a visual aid for the jury to reinforce what he was saying. It looked like this:

EXPERT'S ACTIONS	EXPERT'S WORDS
Always have two security officers	Don't need two clerks
Training important	No training required
Never approach—call police	Okay to approach

This simple approach, built around a consistent theme that "Actions speak louder than words" helped the jury understand the hypocrisy of the expert and to reject his testimony.

Figure out the fertile areas where the defense expert is vulnerable to attack. Because he will always know more than you about this area, stay out of his playground and focus on the reasons he may be mistaken or bending the facts to fit his theory. If possible, build your questions around a theme that will be easy for the jury to remember.

Finally, if his opinion is not based in science and will only confuse the jury, you can do what we did in Elizabeth Garcia's case and try to exclude it entirely.

16

EXCLUDING THE ALLSUP'S EXPERT PROFILER'S HOCUS-POCUS

If a corporation decides to spend its money fighting its deceased worker's children rather than improving safety for its other workers, how can it obscure its own misconduct? By hiring an expert witness to place the blame on someone else.

The Allsup's attorneys found that expert witness in an ex–FBI agent profiler named Gregg McCrary, who, as he had done in other security cases where women were abducted or raped, blamed Elizabeth Garcia.

According to McCrary, because Elizabeth Garcia was such an attractive and vivacious woman, she had attracted an undeterrable stalker. Despite the fact that one of Elizabeth's last acts was to follow Allsup's company protocol for a robbery and push the "No Sale" button on the cash register at 2:24 a.m. and that the cash register drawer was found open with all cash ($12) missing from the drawer, McCrary said the police were wrong when they concluded that the poor security and bad lighting had attracted a methamphetamine-seeking robber. He claimed it was Elizabeth who had brought this upon herself. He said this was an unfore-seeable, victim-targeted crime, and no amount of security or training from Allsup's would have made a difference.

Gregg McCrary

Although he admitted that he had no evidence that the killer, Paul Lovett, knew or had ever met Elizabeth, and that there was no evidence that Elizabeth was being stalked or shadowed by any-one—even her closest friends did not know she had gone to work on the Allsup's graveyard shift—McCrary claimed to be able to determine the intent of the killer by the number of stab wounds on Elizabeth's body. He disagreed with the independent forensic pathologist, Dr. Ross Zumwalt from the New Mexico Office of the Medical Investigator, that the many stab wounds indicated an inexperienced or first-time killer who was freaked out when the victim did not die immediately. McCrary said the viciousness of the attack indicated that the killer knew Elizabeth, was stalking her, and nothing would have deterred him.

And no, he didn't need to interview the killer to determine his intent, because killers can't be trusted to tell you the truth.[1]

If all of this sounds like hogwash, it was. Although criminal profilers, like psychics, make for good television, there is little scientific basis for their guesses about an unknown suspect's

---

1. After the trial was over, we heard that McCrary had contacted the killer in prison pretending to be a researcher and tried to interview him. Because his criminal case was still on appeal, the man refused to talk to him. McCrary never told him he was an expert witness for Allsup's in the civil case.

characteristics. A 2007 *New Yorker* article, "Dangerous Minds" by Malcolm Gladwell, exposed the flimflam of profiler "opinions." Describing the techniques laid out by magician Ian Rowland in his book *The Full Facts Book of Cold Reading*, the article compared profiler predictions to those of psychics in using the following scam techniques, among others:

- **The Barnum Statement**—making many general predictions about the subject (for example, "single, loner, left-handed, moustache, highly educated"), then, when the actual subject is captured, taking credit for those that are correct and ignoring the majority of the predictions that are incorrect.

- **The Rainbow Ruse**—a statement that credits the subject with a personality trait and its opposite (for example, "He can be quiet, but will speak up for himself when needed").

- **The Fuzzy Fact**—making an assertion so general that it leaves plenty of room to be developed into something more specific (for example, "I see a connection with a warm place").

Add guesses based on statistical information about the kinds of people who usually commit a crime (for example, young males between the ages of eighteen and thirty), and the psychic scammers or criminal profilers can sound as if they know what they are talking about, all without a shred of scientific evidence to back up their predictions.[2]

Mr. Gladwell's article discussed scientific studies conducted by Laurence Alison at the University of Liverpool, which disputed the accuracy of profiler predictions under various circumstances:

- When a profiler presents unverifiable, vague, or contradictory predictions to a group of experienced law enforcement officers, the officers find the predictions highly accurate when compared with the actual verified killer. But the officers also find the predictions highly accurate when the traits are exactly the opposite of the actual killer.

---

2. Malcolm Gladwell, "Dangerous Minds," *New Yorker*, Nov. 12, 2007.

◆ There is no scientific basis or support for the FBI profiler's delineation of "organized" vs. "disorganized" traits in predicting what kind of person a serial killer will be. In fact, most crimes are almost always a mixture of different kinds of human behavior.

◆ The majority of predictions by well-known FBI profilers on famous cases—including the team of profilers who came up with a series of guesses for the recently captured BTK (Bind, Torture, Kill) serial murderer, who was captured in 2005—are flat wrong.

The problem with the testimony of profilers, like the testimony of psychics or tarot card readers, is that despite the lack of a scientific, or solid, basis for their opinions, some jurors find comfort in believing there are those who can lay hands on the crime scene and predict unknowable things about the killer. More worrisome is that the series of tricks and techniques described in Mr. Gladwell's article, "when put together in skillful combination, can convince even the most skeptical observer that he or she is in the presence of real insight."

For us, the scariest part of this research was learning that McCrary had been allowed to testify about the intent of criminals in numerous other civil and criminal cases in federal and state courts around the country. He said this testimony had only successfully been challenged and excluded as unscientific one time— in the United States Supreme Court case of *Daubert v. Merrell Dow Pharmaceuticals, Inc.*[3]

Our office went to work putting our one hundred hours of investigation into McCrary. We began contacting lawyers across the country that had faced McCrary across a courtroom. They shared depositions, trial testimony, and transcripts of this expert, whose big claim to fame was repeatedly speculating to the media about JonBenet Ramsey's killer.

The great Alabama trial lawyer David Marsh was particularly helpful, sending us his "Bible" on McCrary. It was packed with

---

3. *Daubert v. Merrell Dow Pharmaceuticals, Inc.*, 509 US 57, 113 S.Ct. 2786, 2796, 125 L.Ed.2d 469 (1993).

television interviews and transcripts of paid testimony on behalf of businesses in security cases that sounded eerily familiar to his opinion in our case: that this particular criminal had targeted the victim and was undeterrable. These invaluable materials included a case in which, after a woman jumped through a glass window from the second story of an apartment complex to escape her nocturnal rapist, McCrary testified that either she had attracted the "stalker" herself or the sex was consensual.

Our independent research revealed that McCrary's memory that he had only been excluded once from testifying about what was in the mind of a killer because it was not scientifically valid was inaccurate.[4] It was not just one court that had excluded his brand of "profiler" testimony on the unknowable intent of a criminal suspect. We found at least five cases where his testimony had been excluded, determined to be reversible error, or withdrawn by courts in Tennessee, Ohio, and Alabama. In *State v. Garcia*,[5] the Ohio Court of Appeals found it was improper to admit McCrary's testimony about the motive of the accused. Ohio defense counsel Dan Doughten had the same experience we had in our deposition—McCrary failed to reveal the other cases in which his testimony had been excluded or limited on *Daubert* grounds.

After completing our investigation, we filed a motion to exclude McCrary's testimony on the basis that it was not grounded in science, was unreliable, and would confuse, rather than assist, the jury.[6]

At the pretrial *Daubert* hearing before Judge Raymond Ortiz (one of the state's smartest, most thoughtful judges and an excellent poet), McCrary tried a dodge to avoid having his nonscientific opinions excluded. He was not, he now claimed, testifying

---

4. *McConnell v. Allsup's*, Gregg McCrary deposition, December 12, 2007, p. 181.

5. *State v. Garcia*, 2002-Ohio-4179, Court of Appeals of Ohio, Eighth District (August 15, 2002).

6. A copy of this motion, called "Motion Gregg McCrary," is available to download at http://www.trialguides.com/resources/downloads/changing-laws.

as a profiler, even though that was the title on his website for his brand of expertise. He now claimed he was coming in as an *accident scene reconstructionist*, to merely testify about what he could deduce from the crime scene evidence. Although no longer saying he could divine the intent of a criminal he had not interviewed, the resulting testimony would be the same. That is, that the multiple stab wounds were the result of rage and indicated the killer may have known and targeted Elizabeth rather than robbing the place.

Judge Ortiz was not fooled. Recognizing that this testimony might confuse or mislead the jury, he issued an order excluding this speculative testimony at trial.

In response to our questions during the hearing about not disclosing all the other cases where his testimony had been excluded, McCrary claimed that the attorneys who hired him never advised him that the court had excluded his testimony. We made sure to send Mr. McCrary a copy of Judge Ortiz's order so he could never again claim he didn't know about the exclusion of his testimony, in our case and in the other cases in which he had testified.[7]

After his testimony was excluded, McCrary was not called as an expert witness at trial. Instead, Allsup's brought another security expert to trial, a man named Merlyn D. Moore.

Merlyn D. Moore

---

7. A copy of Judge Ortiz's order, called "Order Judge Ortiz about Gregg McCrary," is available at http://www.trialguides.com/resources/downloads/changing-laws.

Mr. Moore testified that, regardless of the crime history of other stores, if a convenience store didn't have a robbery for two years, it was okay to stop spending money on security. It was okay to stop maintaining the lights, to take down a bullet-resistant enclosure, and to stop fixing the alarm system. He said it was perfectly permissible for a business to sit down and calculate, based on the crime history of the individual store, the risk of whether it was worth spending money on security. The term he used was *calculated risk*.

That term became the heading and theme for his cross-examination at trial after I heard a story from a good friend and former public defender, Stacey Ward. She told me that her father, after serving in World War II, had come to hate the term. It was what the officers used to explain why they were asking the enlisted men to run up a hill into withering machine-gun fire. The generals would often explain that they had calculated the risk of success and decided the assault was worth it. Stacey's father told her that someone's view of calculated risk was different depending on whether he was doing the calculating or whether he was taking the risk.

The idea of calculated risk was similar to the proposal made by the clerks from Allsup's Tucumcari Store No. 58. Among the suggestions in the letter they wrote to the state Environmental Improvement Board was the following:

> We would like to see the home office people or part of them to work in a store to see what they are asking people to do and see if they feel safe working a graveyard by themselves. This might give them new perspective on the safety of the stores at night.[8]

Based on the idea that your acceptance of calculated risk depends on whether you were on the front lines or back in the

---

8. Employees of Allsup's Store No. 58 to New Mexico Environmental Improvement Board, January 12, 1995, attached to Serious Violation issued to Allsup's on January 11, 1995, after the death of Elizabeth Williams. You can download a copy of this letter, called "Letter to New Mexico EIB," at http://www.trialguides.com/resources/downloads/changing-laws.

home office, these are the questions I asked the Allsup's security expert, Merlyn Moore, on cross-examination:

Q: What you're talking about really, Dr. Moore, is something called calculated risk, and that's kind of what you did; is that right?

A: To a certain extent, yes . . .

Q: Is it all right for companies to look at the crime history of a store, of a particular store, in trying to make that calculation?

A: Oh, absolutely. . . .

Q: If you know that there's crime in a store or a big risk in a store, it would never be appropriate to say, "I'm not going to put that in just because of the money." Is that right?

A: Oh, I would agree with you there, yes.

Q: There's no such thing as an unintentional decision, is there? The word decision implies that you think about it; isn't that correct, Dr. Moore?

A: Decisions are all about alternative choices, and based on the data you look at, you're going to choose one of those choices.

Q: Yes, sir.

A: And so that's really what companies are doing.

Q: Yes, sir.

A: They get the information, and then they make the decision.

Q: And the decision is always an intentional decision rather than an unintentional decision?

A: I would agree with that . . .

Q: [S]omeone in Allsup's made a calculated decision about what kinds of security to put in their stores; is that right?

A: I would assume so.

Q: And whoever that person was, whether it was Lonnie Allsup or Mark Allsup or someone else, he was deciding how much money would be spent on security across the board in all stores; is that right?

A: I would assume that to be true as well.

Q: There is a problem, isn't there, if the person calculating—doing the calculating is the person who benefits from not putting money into security, isn't there?

A: There can or cannot be . . .

Q: The people taking the risk and bearing the risk of this decision were not the people back in the corporate office making a decision about how much to spend for security, and I mean the direct risk. . . . The person who was putting their life on the line every night in these stores was not that corporate executive. It was the minimum-wage worker who was working alone on the midnight shift; isn't that right, sir?

A: That was the individual who was working on the late night shift.

Q: Yes. And the money savings on security didn't get passed on to them in the form of a bonus if you work the midnight shift, did it?

A: No.

Q: In fact, they still made the minimum wage even when working the midnight or graveyard shift, didn't they?

A: Yes, they did . . .

Q: The minimum-wage clerks who worked on the graveyard shift, where 92 percent of the crime was happening in these Allsup's stores, didn't get hazardous duty pay for working the midnight shift, did they, sir?

A: I really don't know. I don't know that I've seen any documents whether they were getting any additional pay.[9]

Although Mr. Moore was a very accomplished and smooth expert witness, using the theme he had inadvertently provided me with—calculated risk—allowed a cross-examination that helped illuminate what was really going on in the Allsup's corporation for the jury. Look for similar gifts in your experts' depositions and build a truth-exposing cross-examination around what they give you.

9. Partial Transcript of Proceedings, *McConnell v. Allsup's*, April 3, 2008, Cross-examination of Merlyn Moore, p. 37–45.

17

What Should I Wear in Court?

The number one question women around the country ask me is, "What should I wear in court?"

This is not as inconsequential a question as it sounds. In the modern American courtroom, the uniform for men has been set for over one hundred years—the suit and tie.

When women first stepped into court, the only clothing example they had was that of their male counterparts. So they dressed just like men, down to the little rosettes cinched around their necks as substitute ties. There were few manufacturers that made suits to fit a woman's body. Adding to the confusion about how to dress, the all-male judiciary in most places required women to wear skirts and would throw them out of court if they showed up in the trousers that their male counterparts wore.

At the time I started practicing, over thirty years ago, I followed the prevailing wisdom. I dutifully purchased two dark—one black, one blue—boxy skirt suits, four white blouses, a couple of "girly" rosette ties, and a pair of black pumps with low one-inch heels. To complete the transformation into the illusion of a male lawyer, I learned to bind my long blonde hair into a severe bun.

This was how I dressed for work my first two years as a lawyer. Then, one day, I was videotaped coming out of court on a criminal case I was prosecuting. When broadcast on the nightly news, I did not recognize the person in the news story. Although easily identifiable as a lawyer, the creature on the television was nothing like me. Stripped of anything that would identify me as a woman, at twenty-seven years old, I looked like an old daguerreotype of my great-grandfather—just in a skirt.

Arghhh! Women have so many more options than men do when it comes to dressing in the courtroom. Even the standby suit requires a choice between pants or skirts, black or color, sheer, shiny, or matte blouses, flats or heels (one-inch, two-inch, four-inch, platform, peeptoe). Throw in our options of dresses, skirts (in a myriad of lengths, styles, and materials) and accessories, and the cornucopia of choices rapidly becomes overwhelming. No wonder Hillary Clinton kept going back to the reliable black pantsuit (although her clothing repertoire improved greatly after becoming secretary of state).

DRESSING SEXY IN THE COURTROOM

Sex sells. Admit it. Influenced by a barrage of retouched, high-gloss imagery, consciously or unconsciously, we have all purchased colognes, lipstick, deodorant, jeans—stonewashed, then dark blue, then skinny—all based on the advertising promise that those things would make us more attractive to a potential partner.

For me it turns out it was all wasted money. To capture the heart of my race-car-driving husband, all I really needed was to dab a little motor oil behind each ear.

If it works so well in advertising, will dressing sexy work in the courtroom?

No.

Tight pencil skirts and low-cut, cleavage-revealing blouses may make good television (*The Good Wife*, *Ally McBeal*, and *Boston Legal*), but are the kind of dynamite that may blow up your case in the courtroom (or the workplace).

Confused? Of course. On one hand, our parents encouraged us as women to educate ourselves, to make our way into the workplace, and to be anything we wanted to be. On the other hand, there was and is the constant drumbeat from women's magazines, movies, music, television, and advertising that women must not only be attractive, but must be sexy. No matter how much we try to throw off the shackles of society's expectations, we carry those expectations around with us.

Sexy or Smart?

Ask yourself in any situation, if you had to choose only one, would you prefer for others to see you as being smart or being sexy?

Smart is better. Even with the invention of Botox, smart lasts longer than your looks. Smart helps you navigate the world, make wise decisions, succeed in business, and tell a good story. Despite knowing all that, no matter how high we climb or how much we accomplish, why is there still this nagging little voice asking, "Yes, you are the president of a Fortune 500 company, but do you still look hot?"

The answer comes from the biological endgame, the real reason for looking "hot." Biologically speaking, we make ourselves sexually attractive to attract a mate. The mating game is not a cooperative team sport. It is a contest where you are competing with the other women in the room.

Why is that a problem? In the courtroom, as a plaintiffs' lawyer, you can't win unless most of the jury is with you. If you appeal to just one group—men or gay women—using your sexuality, you are alienating another group: the straight women you need for your verdict. In politics, you can win with 51 percent of the vote (or less if the electoral college breaks your way). In trial, 51 percent wins you nothing but the nightmare prospect of having to try the case all over again.

As a woman trial lawyer and businesswoman, you have to choose. When you walk into the courtroom (or boardroom), do you want the people to shake your hand or pat you on the posterior? You can't have both.

DEVELOPING MY OWN STYLE

After barely recognizing myself on TV, I knew I had to change. With no female role models that early in my career, I began fumbling around to find a style that was true to who I really was. As a former cowgirl, it began with long skirts or dresses, and boots.

The response from the jurors to the new, real me was immediate and positive. It turns out people don't like lawyers. Dressed like a woman, I no longer looked like a typical "lawyer," but more like one of the jurors. Coupled with speaking in common parlance rather than highfalutin lawyer language, I found jurors looking to me as the go-to person in the courtroom to explain what was going on and what they should do.

It turns out that the courtroom style I stumbled upon, in a time where there were no role models for women lawyers, has been tested in a positive way by Atlanta lawyer Don Keenan and his traveling team of researchers. After determining that the public and our jurors detest lawyers, the research subjects were asked what they would like lawyers to be. Their answer? They would like them to be "caring teachers."

This is great news for women lawyers. Almost all of the teachers we remember from our elementary school years were women. If it is true to your personality, model yourself on those caring teachers (dresses and sweaters à la Michelle Obama). So long as you match your surface look with an honest and teaching approach in your trial presentation, it will give you more believability in the courtroom over the men in suits or the sex-kitten defense lawyer with a thigh-high slit in her tight skirt and skyscraper stilettos. (See confessional below.)

Not only will you have the winning edge with the jury, but you may learn an important life lesson. You are most attractive when leading with your intelligence and your passion for your clients rather than overtly displaying your body parts.

SLAVE SHOES OR POWER PUMPS?

On the issue of sky-high stilettos, I have a confession. My one weakness in the courtroom is terrific high-heeled shoes.

Okay, okay, I know all about the research from podiatrists who say these are bad for your feet and your posture. I know some of my female friends find heels an anathema to feminism. One woman I know, who only ever wears sensible brogues and trousers, calls heels "slave shoes," designed to hobble women and keep them from running away, which turn them into ineffectual sex objects.

Perhaps I have been brainwashed by *Vogue*, *Glamour*, and Lady Gaga into embracing these "chains" on my feet, but I still love and wear high heels in the courtroom. It's not just that I like the way they look. The logical lawyer side of my brain has come up with a completely plausible reason for the continued self-abuse of my feet—the size of the lecterns in the courtroom. Every one of these giant blocks of wood has been built for male-sized lawyers. The result for us shorter women is that, if we are required to stay behind the lectern, as is the rule in most federal courts, we become nothing more than a floating head on top of the wood block.

With 90 percent of my body hidden behind the lectern, I am robbed of the ability to communicate through hand gestures and body language. Wearing heels makes me tall enough to see over the lectern and makes my hands visible and useful again. Better still is moving out from behind the lectern (which is a barrier to any real communication), where the women jurors can appreciate those great "power pumps" I'm wearing. That's right, modern women wear great shoes for each other, not for the men in their lives.

The key to the clothing you choose for the courtroom is to be true to yourself, with the understanding that everything you wear and everything you do is being scrutinized by the people who will judge you, your client, and your case. Jurors can spot a phony a mile off. That holds true for not just you, but for your clients and witnesses as well. If you expect your witnesses to bring their authentic selves to the courtroom, you need to do the same.

18

SPEAKING TRUTH TO POWER

If it works correctly, the courtroom is a crucible where the truth will finally be revealed. Although it takes too long to get to court (for the Garcia family it was nearly six years), once you are there, the people you represent, no matter their station in life, have an opportunity found in few places in the world and that has been rarely available throughout human history. They can take the witness stand and speak truth to the powerful.

Testifying is a nerve-racking experience for everyone but those who do it for a living like expert witnesses and law enforcement officers, the worst of whom learn to *testilie* so smoothly it is hard to reveal their dishonesty through cross-examination. Even for someone like Victorina Garcia, who had worked in government and occasionally spoke in staff meetings, getting up in front of a group of twelve strangers and a judge to talk about the worst thing that had ever happened in her life was a daunting thought.

How do you prepare someone to testify in a way that reveals the truth?

The popular misconception is that we write out a script of questions and answers and then practice them over and over with each witness the way some big-firm defense lawyers do, sometimes videotaping the practices to have a trial consultant go over the "game films" and change how the witness behaves. There is a problem with this approach. The truth cannot be scripted.

A large insurance company tried the scripted-testimony approach with its upper-level management in an employment discrimination case we tried in federal court. Every time I asked the vice president of the company a question when he was testifying before the jury, rather than make eye contact with me, he would assiduously turn his whole body to the jury and answer the question before turning back to me. I guessed that this unnatural way of having a conversation was something that someone had recently taught him. So, in front of the jury, I asked him whether he had been practicing his testimony with someone, perhaps on videotape.

His eyes grew wide and he looked shell-shocked. This, apparently, was not one of the questions the jury consultant had prepared him for. For the first time he didn't turn to the jury to answer, but looked pleadingly to the attorneys at the defense table. When they couldn't answer for him, he revealed his true nature. He lied.

"Why, no," he said, "I haven't been practicing my testimony."

Of course, ethical attorneys cannot let an untruth like that go uncorrected.

After the lunch break, the senior defense attorney approached me and said, "We can't figure out how you found out about this, but he did practice his testimony on videotape with a jury consultant. We're going to have to let the judge know to correct this in the record."

Upon hearing about the deception, the federal judge had a novel solution. He asked whether the videotape of the testimony practice still existed. When he found out that it did, he recessed the trial and ordered the defendants to produce the tape to me by 5:00 p.m., and to bring the witness back the next morning for me to cross-examine with what I found on the videotape.

"Of course," said the judge with a twinkle in his eye, "if the case settles this afternoon before you turn over the videotape, the cross-examination will not have to occur tomorrow."

The case settled that afternoon.

I cannot tell you for a fact that the Allsup's defense lawyers prepared their witnesses by practicing over and over again with a jury consultant. I can tell you that they chose not to bring CEO of Allsup's, Lonnie Allsup—the man who could not remember Elizabeth Garcia's name in his deposition, to the courtroom. Instead, they chose Barbara Allsup to sit in the courtroom during trial and to testify as the corporate representative.

Mrs. Allsup had been made over by the time she came to court. She no longer wore the large diamond ring she had on the morning of her deposition. She came to the courtroom with none of the trappings of her massive wealth, no expensive handbag or clothing. She looked like a kindly grandmother rather than one of the owners of a convenience store empire.

On direct examination, for the first time in six years of litigation, Barbara Allsup managed to tear up, cry, and say she was sorry for Elizabeth's death. This is something she had never done in her deposition or privately with the Garcia family.

The one inkling we had that a jury consultant was working with Mrs. Allsup came after she testified in the afternoon, then came back in the morning. Apparently, someone on the shadow jury (which was debriefed each night by the defense's jury consultant) didn't like this portion of her direct testimony or didn't like her. The next day, when she resumed the witness stand, she tried to change her demeanor and made a comment from the stand that perhaps she was coming across in a way she didn't intend.

The problem with scripting the answers for a client and having them play a role, like that of a kindly grandmother, is that actors are not subject to cross-examination. Once we scratched her surface with probing questions, she quickly revealed her true self: the calculating business owner who kept the $2.2 million a year—the cost of adding a second clerk in all her stores and protecting her company's minimum-wage workers—for herself and her husband.

During direct examination, she even tried to take credit for the fact that by the time of trial the Allsup's stores in Hobbs had two clerks on duty for the graveyard shift and had installed security cameras. This opened the door to our cross-examination that Allsup's hadn't had a sudden epiphany that it should do the right thing and make clerks safe by adding a second worker and security cameras. Allsup's had only done so when the new New Mexico Environmental Improvement Board's regulations forced it to. These were the regulations the Garcia family and the families of other clerks had lobbied for over the convenience store industry's objections.

We brought out that Allsup's had not been happy about the regulations, as evidenced by the fact they didn't add a second clerk on the graveyard shift until the regulations went into effect in February 2005. Just as Mark Allsup had told Chief Knott, Allsup's believed state regulators should not be able to tell them how to run their business.

Remember that Allsup's contributed to fund an appeal challenging the regulations to the New Mexico Supreme Court and made $82,328 in political contributions in 2006 to try to get New Mexico legislators to overturn the regulations. Instead of protecting their clerks, they chose to spend the money on fighting the safety regulations. Most telling of all about Allsup's true intent was the fact that they only made these changes in New Mexico, where it was now required by law. In Texas, where there was no EIB regulation, Allsup's made no changes. They continued to have clerks work alone on the graveyard shift without security cameras in the 184 convenience stores in the Lone Star State.[1]

None of our witnesses in the case were given a script or told how to answer any question. They all wore their own clothing, and the only direction we gave them was to dress like they were going to church or another important event. If they were not the kind of person who was comfortable wearing a suit and tie, they were told they should not wear one in court.

All of our trial witnesses looked like what they were. Dr. Richard Swanson came in his own tweedy sport coat, looking like the college professor he had been. Eva Pellissier, the former Allsup's

---

1. There were 184 convenience stores in Texas at the time of the trial in 2008. There may be more now.

employee, came in a long skirt and modest blouse that barely hid the scar on her neck from where her throat had been cut. Tan, fit, and impeccably dressed in a suit and tie, Wayland Clifton still had the bearing of a Florida police chief. Still in prison, Brian Nash appeared on videotape in his blue prison jumpsuit.

Wearing the clothes from her own closet, *real* grandmother Victorina Garcia was her authentic self on the witness stand. Dignified, soft-spoken, and intelligent, she described all her daughter had meant to the family and how Elizabeth's death had affected the three children. Victorina spoke about how Elizabeth had been into health food and made sure the children always ate plenty of fruits, vegetables, grains, and nuts. She sheepishly acknowledged her own shortcomings when it came to a healthy diet, admitting that the children had to get used to eating her beans and tortillas rather than granola.

Throughout it all, as she told story after story about her daughter and grandchildren, although her eyes grew misty, the woman who had suffered the most, and without financial help had voluntarily taken in the three children, did not break down and cry like Mrs. Allsup. Every word she spoke rang absolutely true.

Even though the motto for our lawyers is that "there is no crying in court," I'm not sure that, faced with the loss of my own daughter, I could have done the same.

19

THERE IS NO CRYING IN COURT

Just like coach Jimmy Dugan (played by Tom Hanks) plaintively wails to his sobbing female player in the movie *A League of Their Own*, there is no crying in baseball and there is no crying in court.

When a judge starts screaming at you and then dismisses your case, it does not give your client any comfort if you begin sobbing into your hankie.

When the jury convicts your innocent client of a crime he did not commit, and the marshals come to handcuff him and take him off to jail, it will not make him feel any better if his lawyer dissolves into a puddle of tears.

Your clients come to you when the worst thing in their lives has happened. Your clients and their families are counting on you, their chosen champion, to either make it better or, sometimes, just to walk with them through the hellish nightmare that is a criminal or civil trial. You are there to help them, to be the one person in the courtroom who is on their side. It does not help them if you fall apart.

Nor does a crying lawyer generate sympathy for someone who has been horribly injured or for the family of someone who has been killed. Modern jurors believe that crying lawyers, particularly plaintiffs' lawyers who are representing injured people, are only crying as a ruse to manipulate the jury to award more money. No matter how genuine your feelings or your tears, the jury will believe they are false.

The One Time I Cried in Court

Jason Seifried

The only time I cried in the courtroom was during a civil trial involving the death of a young man named Jason Seifried. He was beaten to death at the age of fifteen by another student at his high school in the middle of the day. The beating took place outside a classroom and the teacher inside heard it but did not take the time to stop the fight.[1]

Jason had reported to high school administrators that the other boy was threatening him, but no one alerted his parents,

---

1. *Seifried v. Rizzo*, New Mexico Second Judicial District Court, case number D-202-CV-199207944.

Mark and Starr, about the ongoing conflict. Jason was a remarkable young man who had been riding horses and competing in rodeos since he was five years old. One of my favorite pictures of him was at age seven or eight, holding a saddle he had just won that looked as big as he was.

The crying came in closing argument and was not planned or staged in any way—I am not that good an actress and have never been able to cry on purpose. We had admitted into evidence a lined spiral notebook from one of Jason's English classes. It contained several assignments that required him to write out, in the scrawling, cursive handwriting of a teenage boy, his hopes, dreams, and plans for the future.

I told the jury that after all the witnesses they'd heard discuss the bullying and the dangerous hallways of Los Lunas High School, the one person they hadn't gotten to hear from was Jason himself. I pulled up a chair in the middle of the courtroom, opened up the spiral notebook, and began to read aloud, in the first person, the simple dreams of this wonderful young man.

From his handwritten essays, written one year before his death:

> Hi, my name's Jason Seifried and I'm here to introduce myself. I first got interested in rodeo when I was three-and-a-half or four. Jake Barnes, the world champion team roper, and his sister taught me to ride and then to rope. When I was five I won my first saddle which led to six or seven more and one state 4-H championship.
>
> My favorite music groups are all country singers and Whitesnake. My favorite animals are my two dogs . . . who I don't think of as animals, but I think of as friends and partners.
>
> My idle [sic] is Ned Tietjen. He is my idle [sic] because of his great roping ability and for his courage and stamina. When he was first starting to rodeo he and Janet, his wife, went alongside the roads to pick up cans to cash in so he could get gas money and so

he could pay the next rodeo's entry fees . . . Now he is the two-time NMRA state all-around champion and is trying to make it three this year.

If I suddenly won $500,000 . . . first, I would buy several sections of land, somewhere in Southwestern Texas to farm or ranch on. I would buy an industrial sized arc welder, a John Deere front-end loader, and a small tractor. Next I would buy material to build a ropin' arena identical to Jimmie Cooper's and 110 head of calves and steers.

Ten years from now, I'll probably be going to Sul Ross or Eastern N.M. State and probably be college rodeoing. After that, I might go pro rodeoing, if my knee permits. And if my knee doesn't permit, I might buy some property and farm it, and raise a family.

Well, this concludes my introduction. I hope you've enjoyed it. Thank you.

As I read, in the first person, in his own voice, from the teen-age-boy scrawl in his school-lined notebook, the testimony of his father, Mark Seifried, came flooding back to me. Mark, a stoic cowboy from whom Jason had learned how to be a man, felt he had to be the strong one in the family. After the loss of their only child, he held himself together for his wife, Starr. He did not cry at the news of his son's death. He did not cry at the funeral. He did not cry until two years after Jason's death, when he was driving down the highway and saw a bumper sticker on the car ahead of him. It said, "Ask me about my grandchildren." Mark, this big, strapping boulder of a man, suddenly realized he would never have any grandchildren. He pulled his truck to the side of the road and wept, alone in his vehicle, for forty-five minutes.

I almost made it through the reading, but when I got to Jason's plans for what he would be doing ten years from now, I was overwhelmed by this great loss to his parents and our community. Like Mark, I broke down in tears. It was this breakdown that the evening news filmed and played on TV.

How did that strike the viewing public? One week after the trial, I received a call from a new potential client, a man who had a contract dispute between his business and another business. "I saw you crying on the news," the potential new client said. "I want to hire you so you can do the same thing for me in my contract case."

I did not take his case, but his call taught me that no matter how sincere your tears are in the courtroom, some people will believe that you staged them and can repeat them.

Our *Seifried* trial ended in a hung jury. Fortunately, it was nine to three in our favor (we needed only one more juror, a total of ten, to win the case). Shortly afterward, the case settled and Mark and Starr used the money to fund scholarships for other kids who were interested in 4–H and rodeo.

How to Keep from Crying

How do you keep from crying in front of the jury when you are dealing with the saddest facts imaginable in a case?

You cry the first day your client tells you about their lost child. You cry when you visit their home to see that, months or sometimes years after the child's death, her bedroom remains untouched, the same as it was the day she died. You cry at night when you are preparing your witnesses to testify at trial. And if you are still not cried out by the time you walk into the courtroom, you pinch yourself or bite the inside of your cheek until it bleeds to keep from crying in front of the jury before the verdict comes in.

There was a lot of cheek biting in Elizabeth Garcia's case.

The hardest moment for me was when Elizabeth's younger brother, Antonio "Tito" Garcia, testified how he got a call at about 3:00 a.m. from a friend who had stopped by the unexpectedly empty store. Tito left Elizabeth's sleeping children with another friend and sped to the Allsup's on the edge of town. There, on the counter, was the open book from the class Elizabeth had just started at community college. There, on the floor, were her purse and all her belongings.

He ran through the store, calling her name, searching the bathrooms, the cooler, out back by the garbage cans, hoping, hoping that maybe she had fallen and hurt herself. His heart sank with each step he took, each place that turned up empty, each unanswered call of his sister's name. He kept thinking this couldn't be happening, but the bad dream only grew worse as the night progressed. No one had seen or heard from her. A search of the surrounding area in the dark turned up nothing. The family gathered, with Victorina driving up from Roswell. An all-consuming dread settled over the house, which only grew worse after the law enforcement officer arrived to confirm the worst with just three words, "Elizabeth is dead."

By the end of his testimony, the inside of my cheek was raw.

20

Seeking Justice, Not Sympathy, in Elizabeth Garcia's Case

Knowing that modern jurors suspect lawyers will try to manipulate them by playing on their emotions, we did everything we could to make sure that did not happen in Elizabeth Garcia's case. Throughout the case, we let the jurors know we were seeking justice, not sympathy.

It started with the horrific, bloody pictures that police took at the scene of Elizabeth Garcia's murder in that empty field.

Because Paul Lovett had never killed anyone before, this death was particularly brutal. First-time killers are surprised when murder is not as quick and antiseptic as it looks on television or in the movies. On the screen it is usually one quick stab with a knife and the person falls dead to the ground. In real life, even if you stab someone in the heart, it takes minutes to bleed out, particularly if the person is struggling to survive and get back to her children.

After Lovett stuck a knife into Elizabeth's chest, she kept breathing and moving. He stabbed her over and over again to make her stop—almost thirty times in her chest and, when she flipped over and tried to crawl away, her lifeblood flowing out into the dirt, he thrust the knife into her back another twenty-six times. Frantic at the last gurgling noises she was still making, he finally cut her throat.[1]

Your first instinct might be to find the worst of these nightmare photos and blow them up as large as possible on a courtroom screen so that the jury could see what had happened with their own eyes. In this case that just felt wrong, even disrespectful of Elizabeth's struggle to survive. What, then, should we do with this evidence?

The answer came from a remarkable Iowa lawyer, one of the first successful women plaintiffs' lawyers in the country and one of my mentors, Roxanne Barton Conlin. Texas titan Jim Perdue echoed this answer. Roxanne had a counterintuitive suggestion. Have the forensic pathologist catalog each injury using an outline diagram of the body, marking and orally describing the photos as he discussed how the murder took place. Then we could admit, but not show, the photos to the jury.

That is exactly what we did. Forensic pathologist Ross Zumwalt described how the murder took place, noting the number and type of injuries. Then, without showing the marked photographs to the jury, we had him place the ten scene photos we had selected into a manila envelope, seal it shut, and mark it "For Damages Only." In closing argument, I told the jury they should only open the envelope if they needed to see the photos to understand what Elizabeth had suffered in order to fairly assess damages.

Later, during deliberations, the jury discussed and voted on whether they should open the envelope at all, finally deciding that they owed Elizabeth Garcia the duty of understanding what she had been through, in that dark field, before they could render a final decision on the case. Around the table, one by one, they solemnly passed the photos, holding Elizabeth's broken body gently in their own hands, some tearing up at what they saw, then resealed the photos in the envelope. They told us later it was a

---

1. Paraphrased from *McConnell v. Allsup's,* testimony of Ross Zumwalt, New Mexico Office of the Medical Investigator.

shared moment of profound respect and honor, something that would not have happened if we had scorched their eyes with these gruesome photos on a huge screen.

We also faced the issue of sympathy when it came to deciding whether any of Elizabeth's three children would testify at trial.

Elizabeth was murdered in 2002, but the case didn't go to trial until 2008. Almost six years after their mother's death, Xavier was twelve years old, Jerome was ten, and Cene was nine. One of our claims was the children's loss of consortium or loss of guidance, counseling, and a relationship with their mother. Who better to testify about what the loss of their mother meant to them than the children themselves?

Certainly, it might help the case, but would it help Elizabeth's children?

This question is similar to the one we always ask before taking on a civil rape case—one where we are suing the rapist, or suing the unsafe apartment complex where he serially preyed upon unsuspecting women tenants who had been promised the place was safe for single women.

Rape survivors respond to the trauma of their attack in very different ways—ways that are neither right nor wrong. Some find healing by standing up for themselves, confronting their attacker in criminal court, and putting him behind bars. Other rape survivors try to recover their lost sense of security through self-defense courses, arming themselves with a weapon, or changing their appearance in a way they think will make them unattractive to predators—such as gaining weight, dressing in baggy clothing, or going without makeup. For these women, a civil lawsuit and the prospect of helping protect other women by adding security at the apartment complex, or requiring apartment managers to tell prospective tenants about previous assaults on the property, may further empower them or help them to feel safe.

Other survivors are so devastated they become agoraphobic, retreating from the world, their jobs, their friends, and rarely emerging from their homes. Still others have their worldview so twisted by sexual violence that they seek understanding of the incomprehensible rape by deliberately placing themselves in dangerous situations with unstable men, over and over again, to see if they can achieve a different outcome.

For this second group of more fragile survivors, the civil justice system may actually inflict more harm upon them than the good you might achieve. For them, a lawsuit that drags out over three or four years is like continuously hacking the scab off a deep wound and making it bleed again and again. You can see the flinch in their eyes at the defense lawyer's questions in a day-long deposition, and you can see how they walk out of the room hunched over, beaten again with words rather than fists.

In rape cases, no amount of money or changes can justify ending the case with your client psychologically and emotionally worse off than when she began the litigation. This is why we will not take a case unless the potential client's therapist lets us know whether, with this particular survivor, litigation is more likely to do her good rather than harm.

That was the same question we asked when deciding whether or not to put Elizabeth's kids on the witness stand. Although they had initially had some grief counseling, by the time we came to trial, it was not their counselor but their grandmother, Victorina Garcia, who knew them best. We asked her how they were doing and what she thought would be best for them.

Based on their individual personalities and ages at the time of their mother's death, each child had reacted to the loss of their mother in a different way.

The middle child, Jerome, age five at the time of the murder, had not been able to comprehend what it meant that his mother was dead and had a difficult time remembering her. He dealt with this hole in his memory by scouring the memories of other friends and family members for stories about Elizabeth. What did she like to eat? What did she like to do? How did she laugh? With the answers he got, he created stories about her—about how she was trying to get the kids to eat healthy, cooking wheat germ pancakes rather than burritos for breakfast. How she signed all the Christmas cards and birthday cards she gave out with a combination of their names—LXJC. By force of will and unceasing questions, he made sure he would not forget her. He was eleven years old at the time of trial.

When her mother died, four-year-old Cene had just reached the childhood age of magic and dealt with her mother's death in a charming, magical way—she believed her mother was always there, watching her. When Cene finished a dance recital and a family friend said how sad it was that her mother could not have seen her performance, Cene smiled brightly and said, "She did see it. She was sitting right there," pointing to a seat in the front row. Cene was more right than she knew. She carried her mother everywhere with her, in her own features, hand gestures, and the way she laughed. Cene was ten when we went to trial.

Xavier, or "X," was seven when Elizabeth died. He was the only one of the children who was old enough at the time to realize what it meant that his mother was gone. X was the one Victorina was initially most worried about. From the time he heard the news in the living room and ran out into the yard screaming, he had been screaming inside ever since. He had worked hard to suppress the rage he felt that day. Because he had to be the man of the house and protect and help raise his younger brother and sister, he did not have the luxury of letting it show. Now that he was thirteen and coming out the other side of his anger, although he was the oldest and most capable of testifying, Victorina was concerned that putting him on the stand would dredge up the horror of his loss all over again.

It was this final concern that made the decision for us. No matter how much sympathy it might generate, the kids would not testify. Instead, during her time on the witness stand, we had Victorina talk about her grandchildren and explain the unique ways each had responded to her death. She told how a family member had given her a videotape taken at a wedding, in which Elizabeth was captured saying "I love you" to the married couple (a clip of which we showed at trial).

When Victorina apprehensively showed the clip to the children about a year after her death, they thought Elizabeth's words were meant for them. With no hesitation, Cene spoke right back

Elizabeth Garcia attending a family wedding

to her mother's face on the television. "I love you too," she said. Then, Jerome got up from the couch and kissed the screen.

After Victorina had described each of the children, with permission of the court, we had all three come into the well of the courtroom, where their grandmother introduced each one of them to the jury. They were dressed in their school clothes. When it was Cene's turn to be introduced, she spontaneously stepped forward with a shy "Hi" and waved her hand, an echo of the gesture her mother had made on the video clip shown to the jury. That "Hi" was the only testimony the children gave in the courtroom.

Later that evening, back at the office after a long day at trial, I realized we had done such a good job protecting the children from the litigation that they had never gotten to hear any of the case. When they stopped by to meet up with their grandmother and go to the hotel, I asked her and the children whether they would like to hear what we had discovered about why their mother died. When they said "yes," I pulled out the PowerPoint we had created for opening statement. There in our conference room, around the computer screen, with no audience but Elizabeth's three children, I showed them what we had discovered.

As I told them about all the other mothers who had been killed or hurt working alone in these stores and how the Allsups had broken repeated promises to do something about it, X's shoulders grew more and more tense. And then, I told him, "Of course, when your mom decided to go to school during the day and work at night to support you on January 16, 2002, she didn't have any idea how dangerous the job was."

"She didn't?" X asked.

"No," I said. "They kept that a secret from their employees. If she had known, she would never have gone to work there."

His thin shoulders suddenly relaxed, almost as if some kind of internal fever had broken.

It suddenly occurred to me that, as many children do when a parent dies, X may have been angry at his mother for leaving them, starting with taking a job that took her away in the middle of the night, never to be seen again. Hopefully, learning the history of Allsup's behavior helped him understand to refocus his misplaced anger where it belonged.

Heartbroken all over again by the ripple effect of Elizabeth's death on all those who knew her, I did not shed a single tear . . . until the children left.

21

You Don't Know a Woman until You've Met Her in Court

Being a trial lawyer is one of the greatest jobs in the world. Learning the craft of a trial lawyer gives you the keys to the big power machine. It gives you the ability to start it up and make it work properly, or if someone is abusing the law, it teaches you where to throw the wrench to gum up the works and keep the judicial steamroller from crushing your client.

The Advantage of Being a Woman

Being a woman trial lawyer is an advantage in the courtroom because we are still rare, unexpected, and do not "look like lawyers." So long as you don't squander the initial advantage of being different by revealing yourself to be just another lawyer (or the jurors' misconception of what lawyers are—dishonest, tricky, wordy, and pompous), the jury starts off wanting to believe you.

Even the traditional, stereotypical views of women sometimes act in your favor in the courtroom.

Early in my career, I was trying a case against a particularly obnoxious male opposing counsel. To nearly every question I asked, he loudly and vociferously objected, whether there was a valid legal basis or not. Some of the jurors began shifting in their seats.

His objections grew louder and more frequent, even though the judge was overruling most of them. There was more uncomfortable movement in the jury box. Finally, after a particularly loud objection, one of the male jurors leapt to his feet in the jury box and shouted at my opposing counsel, "Hey, why don't you just leave her alone!"

Needless to say, the objections stopped.

Once, when I was making a closing argument and approached within arm's length of the jury rail, a woman in her eighties leaned out of the jury box to pat me on the arm. Here was a woman who grew up in a time when women were limited in what they were allowed to accomplish, giving me a "You go girl" touch to tell me she was proud of what I was doing.

The best response was the jury that went out and bought me a present in the middle of the trial. Luckily, they discussed whether they should give me the present right after it was purchased—a forbidden jury-to-lawyer contact that would have to have been reported and would have undoubtedly resulted in a mistrial—or to wait until the trial was over. Luckily, they waited until they returned a verdict in my client's favor.

As a cross section of the community, the jury has always been more accepting of women lawyers than others in the legal profession.

Sexism in the Early Years

Change is hard for some people. Not everyone in the white, male-dominated bar welcomed women into the legal system. How I chose to respond to the occasional negative experiences of sexism depended on the intention of the man who was behaving badly.

Was it intentional or just confusion in how to treat women in this new world we were all trying to figure out?

As I was leaving one of my first depositions, an elderly lawyer stepped forward to open the door for me. When I was halfway through the door, a look of panic came across his face and he released the door, which shut on my foot.

"Oh, I'm so sorry," he apologized. "I've been told I'm not supposed to be doing this anymore."

Poor fellow. Politeness is never sexism. He got a pass and a thank you.

Then there was the man who deliberately used sexism as a tactic. In the first deposition in a case, he would always "mistake" the woman lawyer on the other side for the court reporter.

"It's great," I heard him chortling to one of his male cohorts. "The woman gets so mad that she can't focus on what's happening in the deposition." For this type of intentional conduct, I would quickly call the lawyer on his misbehavior, sometimes with a comment about his Neanderthal attitude, and then let it go and focus on doing my job for my client in the case.

The more cases I tried, the more I was able to let this kind of insult and annoyance roll off my back. The reason? The courtroom is the great equalizer. All the prejudices from opposing counsel fall away or work to their disadvantage in front of jurors who understand and support the underdog.

My one horror story from those early years comes from a judge who believed women shouldn't be in the courtroom. State Court Judge Gerald Cole was a nightmare for women lawyers in New Mexico. He realized he couldn't ban women from his courtroom, so he just chose not to acknowledge or address them when they were appearing in front of him. When there was an issue during trial that required a bench conference, he would call the male lawyers, by name, up to the bench, but ignore the woman lawyer.

Worse than the social slights was his tendency to gut the woman lawyer's case by granting unjustified motions to decrease her chances of winning at trial. There is nothing more discouraging than appearing before a judge who has decided to make you lose, either through pretrial motions or taking the case away from you after the verdict.

It is difficult, if not impossible, to change the biases of a prejudiced judge. In the case of Judge Cole, several women lawyers complained to the women judges who served with him in Albuquerque, and those judges raised the issue with Judge Cole. They told him he had to begin acknowledging the women in his courtroom and treat them equally with the men.

His response was to begin calling all of the lawyers in his courtroom by what he deemed was an equal title: "Mister." Needless to say, it was quite confusing to the jurors when he called "Mister" McGinn to the bench. You could see them looking at each other, wondering if there was something they didn't know about me. Was I a cross-dresser? Was the judge senile?

I always wondered whether Judge Cole's misogynistic views carried over to his home life and his wife. After he left the bench for the better-paying job of being a federal hearing officer for disability cases, my question was answered in a horrific way. After years of suffering the same kinds of views we experienced in the courtroom, Judge Cole's wife decided to leave him. He shot her to death and then shot himself.

Luckily, these kinds of judges are few and far between and have become a happily endangered species as they and the corrosive attitudes they carry die off. More women have become judges, society's attitudes have evolved, and most people now accept the presence of women in all aspects of our society.

Yet there are still not enough women in the courtroom, particularly on the defense side. Sometimes defense firms will assign a woman to counteract the "mojo" of a case that our firm brings, but then keep her benched at trial while the men argue in front of the jury. That is what the Allsup's defense team did when the out-of-state lawyers came charging into the courtroom at the last minute.

22

ALLSUP'S ATTEMPT AT SHOCK AND AWE

Just as my friend Paul Luvera had predicted, one week before trial, AIG, which insured the Allsup's corporation, called in its litigation hit team: a large Atlanta law firm now called Weinberg, Wheeler, Hudgins, Gunn & Dial.

Their lead counsel was a lawyer named Y. Kevin Williams, and to counteract the estrogen on our side of the table, they sent a woman lawyer named Carol Michel. Although she proved to be the better lawyer, they had the male lawyer handle the important parts of the trial. A team of researchers and brief writers joined them and were waiting in the wings, along with another large local firm hired to handle any appellate issues.

Between the lawyers who had started the case, the Allsup family's private attorney, and the new group of attorneys, there were usually nine defense lawyers in the courtroom. The same number worked outside the courtroom—researching and filing briefs to which we had to respond.

Sending in a team of hotshot lawyers right before trial was the same shock and awe strategy AIG employed in Paul Luvera's case in Seattle as well as in other cases around the country. The insurance company allowed local counsel to handle cases until right before trial. AIG would monitor the case and, if it wasn't settled and there was a chance of a large verdict, would drop its hit squad on the case right before trial. The idea was to scare the bejesus out of the plaintiffs' lawyers right before trial, either forcing a settlement or discombobulating them so they would falter.

Forewarned is forearmed.

After getting the email from Paul a month before trial, we got copies of some of the motions this firm filed in his case. The one they filed to announce their presence as they entered the case was a motion that would prevent us from telling the real jury that they were using a shadow jury. This was designed to freak out most small-town lawyers like us, who had never even heard of a shadow jury, much less that the other side was going to use such a thing. Rather than just wait for a nuclear bomb to be dropped on our case, we went out and learned everything we could about shadow juries.

Unlike the real jurors, who had no choice about their service and were paid less than minimum wage for the hours they sat in the courtroom, shadow jurors were typically paid $150 a day (or more). Selected from the community by a jury consultant through demographics that matched the real jury, the shadow jurors would come to trial every day and sit in the back of the courtroom listening to opening statements, closing arguments, and all of the evidence.

In order to avoid skewing their opinions, the shadow jury did not know which side had hired them. They had to sign agreements keeping everything confidential. Every night after trial, the jury consultant would feed them dinner and debrief them on their views of the case. The consultant would send them home for the night and then meet with the defense's counsel to let them know what the shadow jury said about their impressions of the witnesses and the evidence. This would allow the defense team to retool or change their case in the middle of trial. Just like they unsuccessfully tried to do with the testimony of Barbara Allsup.

Of course, if the real jury knew this was what the defense lawyers were doing, it would creep them out. That was the reason for the pretrial motion to prevent us from telling the jury who these stalkers were.

Because of the requirement that trials be held in an open public courtroom, many courts around the country feel they have no choice but to let the lawyers bring in whomever they want as shadow jurors. However, the court has the power to insure their presence doesn't affect the deliberations of the real jury.

Our trial was held in the old Santa Fe courthouse, a building in which the pie-shaped courtrooms were the size of a large living room. Although this made for a cozy, intimate feeling, with only three rows of seats in the back of the courtroom, the shadow jurors would be highly visible to the real jurors. It would be impossible not to notice a group of people who came in together every day led by a jury consultant and then sat there taking notes on everything that happened in the courtroom. Since there was only one set of bathrooms on each floor, the shadow jurors and the real jurors would be occupying the same space during breaks, creating a potential for improper contact and contamination.

We put together a response to the motion we suspected was coming, complete with an affidavit from our jury consultant. This affidavit indicated that it would be obvious to the real jurors if the shadow jury traveled as a pack and cause them to wonder who those people in the back of the courtroom were.

One week before trial, on a Friday morning, AIG's Atlanta law firm filed an entry of appearance and the motion about the shadow jury. I imagine they chuckled at the consternation they expected this would engender in our ranks. Within less than an hour, we filed our reply brief, along with the affidavit of our jury consultant, which had been sworn and notarized days before the entry of appearance. Shock and awe back at ya!

After a hearing on our motion, Judge Ortiz allowed the shadow jurors to come into the back of the courtroom, but required that they do so separately, not as a group, so the jury would not be distracted by their presence. He also forbade them to have any contact with the real jurors anywhere in the courthouse.

The other bit of research we did was into Y. Kevin Williams. The firm's glowing description of him on its website only included his successful courtroom ventures and left the impression that he had never lost a case. Was it puffery to lure in clients and intimidate his opponents with his seeming invincibility, or was it real? We wouldn't find out the answer to that question until the case was over.

Since the key to a successful verdict is pretrial preparation, I was left to wonder how Williams, or any lawyer, could come in a week before trial and think he could defend a case he knew nothing about. Since he didn't know anything about New Mexico law, we soon found out that he would argue by having local counsel in the back of the courtroom email arguments and case names to his cell phone, which he read while he argued motions to the court. Since he couldn't read off his cell phone in front of the jury, the only way it was possible to come in and try a case he didn't know a week before trial was if he had a template for similar kinds of cases and tried them the same way over and over again.

It was just like my great-uncle Joe McGinn, a Catholic Maryknoll missionary who, as a young priest, was proselytizing in rural China when the Communists took over the country. In order to cleanse the country of educated professionals who might oppose their regime, within a year of the takeover, a traveling band of prosecutors and witnesses arrived in Father Joe's small village.

In short order, Father Joe was hauled out of his small hut and dragged to the town square with several others, mostly teachers, for a public trial. There, from among the group of portable witnesses, stepped three people he had never met and no one in the village knew. They testified he was guilty of treason because he had spoken to them and said disparaging things about the new government.

Because these same witnesses had been going from town to town relating the exact same story with the exact same words against anyone the Communist Party singled out for trial, the prosecutor's job was easy. He made the same arguments he did everywhere they went together, with the same result—even though these witnesses had never met the people they testified against, everyone was convicted. Father Joe spent eight years in prison before he was released. He spent the rest of his priesthood ministering to the faithful in a parish in Hawaii.

Because of my suspicion that Y. Kevin Williams could only perform as a traveling lawyer if he was trying the same case, we went in search of other workplace violence or lack-of-security cases where he was the lead counsel. In the week before trial, we obtained the transcripts of several of the lack-of-security cases he had tried. Unlike our cases about real live human beings, where we had never made the same argument twice in any opening statement, Williams's opening statements in these cases repeated the same arguments with the same language.

His defense in every one of these cases was that it was a "random, senseless act of violence" that no one could have predicted. He argued that this "random, senseless act" occurred, not because of any defect in security, but because there are just bad people out there in the world whom no one can stop or deter. In his other cases that involved a woman, he argued that it was the woman herself, not the insecure location, who attracted the predator. The argument was the same in each of his security cases. All he had to do as he moved from case to case was change the names of the victims of violence.

How did we use this knowledge in our opening statement?

First, we made our own case. We laid out all the facts we had learned about how Allsup's broke its promises to the families of its murdered workers, broke the security rules that had developed in the convenience store industry to prevent crime, and made Elizabeth Garcia work in a store with a broken alarm system. We told the jury about the warning from Hobbs Police Chief Tony Knott to Mark Allsup a year before Elizabeth went to work, and the views of convenience store robber Brian Nash that Allsup's stores were easy pickings. We let them know about the 1,225 serious crimes in Allsup's stores, 91 percent of which occurred on the graveyard shift with a lone clerk. After telling the jury all the things you have learned in this book, I ended my opening statement by telling the jury what my opponent, Y. Kevin Williams, was about to argue. I used the precise language he'd used in all the other security arguments he had made in the past—and then I answered his arguments. It went like this:[1]

> After I sit down, I expect Mr. Williams is going to get up and say several things on Allsup's behalf.
>
> First, he is going to say this was not a robbery. It was a random, senseless act of violence on a pretty girl. And this is the worst blame of all because what he's saying is, if you're an attractive girl, you're bringing it on yourself. They didn't come for Allsup's. They came for you.
>
> Although it's interesting that [the criminal] never went after her when she was with her family at her house. [The criminal] never went after her when she was working at the AutoZone during the daytime, when she was surrounded by people. It was just here, when she was out on the Lovington Highway by herself.
>
> And they are going to propose to you that it wasn't the money in the register that attracted this late-night predator, it was [Elizabeth] who attracted the predator.
>
> They will ask you this question: How could we possibly have predicted this random senseless act of violence? You're going to hear "random senseless act" a lot. And, you know that might have worked in a case that happened back in 1975, when the first woman was kidnapped from an Allsup's and raped and killed. But after eleven of those people being killed late night on the graveyard shift, after fourteen women being sexually assaulted, taken alone

---

1. All but the first sentence is the actual argument from the trial transcript, *McConnell v. Allsup's*, March 25, 2008.

on the graveyard shift from Allsup's, after sixteen near-death experiences of people, after 1,225 robberies, assaults, and batteries in their stores, they cannot look at you with a straight face and say, "This is a random, senseless act of violence that we couldn't have predicted."

In fact, it was business as usual at Allsup's. And they took the calculated risk that by not putting in security, they wouldn't be held accountable for that.

Ladies and Gentlemen, they staked her out on the Lovington Highway like she was on a silver platter in that store where anyone could do anything to her. They didn't do any of the things they should have done to make her and the store safe. The other things that were done that were the standard in the industry at the time. The things that they'd promised all those people through the years.

At the end of this case, we're going to ask you not just to take care of her family, which is important, but to make sure, by your verdict, that they do the right thing and that this never happens to anybody again. Thank you very much.

By ending opening this way, I had just gutted Y. Kevin Williams's ability to give the standard security spiel he peddled from town to town in all of these security cases. He could not use his go-to phrase, "random, senseless act of violence." He stumbled through the first part of his opening statement, trying and failing to come up with some other phrase or terms that conveyed his argument.

The battle that is trial was on.

23

Finding Courageous Jurors to Be the Heroes and Heroines of Your Case

As the popularity of Congress and the president sinks ever lower in the eyes of the public, a March 3, 2012, survey by the American College of Trial Lawyers found one branch of government in which the public still has faith. When asked, "Which of the three branches of government do you have the most confidence and trust in?" the results were as follows:

Branch of Government	Percentage of Public That Trusts It the Most
Judicial Branch/Courts	61 percent
Executive Branch/President	25 percent
Legislative Branch/Congress	14 percent

I'd like to believe that result is based on our faith in the true heroes and heroines of every case—the jurors.[1] The key to selecting a good jury is not demographics but finding people with the clear-eyed courage to stand up to wrongdoers, no matter how powerful, and make the world a safer place. How do you find these people?

In the early days of my law practice, the general wisdom about jury selection was that you never asked the jury to express any bad opinions or attitudes that might be unfavorable to your case. The thinking in those days was that if one panel member expressed a bad opinion, it would somehow "taint" the rest of the panel. If a bad opinion was stated in open court, a young lawyer was advised to request a mistrial and start over, trying not to tread into that danger-ous territory again. In thirty-four years of practicing law, this was some of the worst advice I ever received about how to select a jury. This approach did not work then and does not work now.

Today's potential jurors come to the courtroom with strong attitudes and opinions about civil cases, plaintiffs' lawyers, and people who sue other people—some correct, and some spawned by industry-funded anti-lawsuit media campaigns. Some of them come to the courtroom with an agenda: that they are not going to be like those other "crazy juries" that gave someone $2 million for spilled coffee. If you don't pull the poisonous views out of "agenda" jurors in open court, they will take them back into the jury room unbeknownst to you and destroy any hope of justice in your case.

In order to see what kind of problematic views you may be facing, go online and check out the anonymous comments fol-lowing any media reports about your case. If there are no stories about your case, find a local or national story about a case similar to your own and track the comments. If that doesn't terrify you into spending quality time on jury selection, nothing will.

If you have a judge who doesn't want to let you have an attorney-conducted voir dire, show him or her the frightening

---

1. For a thoughtful analysis of the juror's elevated place in American jurispru-dence and the lawyer's role as mentor or facilitator in helping jurors on that journey, read Carl Bettinger's excellent book, *Twelve Heroes, One Voice* (Portland, OR: Trial Guides, 2011).

attitudes and opinions you found online. Since jurors want to please the judge, they are less likely to reveal the anonymous, unfiltered views they put on the web if the judge conducts the jury questioning. Only a lawyer, who the jury believes has a lesser status than the judge, might be able to reveal those attitudes. In addition, the lawyer knows more about the case and the problematic issues that might trigger adverse reactions in the jurors.

Your job in jury selection is to identify and eliminate those "agenda" jurors who are there to wreak havoc in the jury room. Jurors who will disregard the judge's instructions and the 51 percent burden of proof and lead the jury to find against your client, no matter the evidence. The only way to identify them is to ask the jurors the things that scare you most—what my friend, Rhode Island lawyer Mark Mandell, calls the "I just can't get over" issues.

There you are standing in front of a group of 30 to 150 complete strangers and you want them to open up to you about their secret, innermost fears and feelings about people who file lawsuits, lawyers, and the legal system. How do you get them talking? In this age of Oprah Winfrey–style talk shows and self-confessions, it is easier than you might think. The key is to focus on what should be the three goals of jury selection:

◆ Gather information.

◆ Remind the jury about truths they already know.

◆ Establish rapport.

GATHER INFORMATION

The more information you know about a potential juror, the better off you are. If you have enough time for a thorough voir dire, you must get sufficient information from a panel member to help you decide whether they are courageous; open- or closed-minded; irreversibly biased against plaintiffs, plaintiffs' lawyers, or lawsuits; capable of empathy; leaders, followers, or somewhere in the mushy middle—where most of our jurors come from. If you are unable to gather information, you will not be able to challenge for cause or intelligently exercise a peremptory challenge. One way is to ask for a supplemental jury questionnaire.[2] The best way is to talk to them face-to-face. Here is how you get them talking.

Ask Open-Ended Questions

If you want jurors to talk to you, you must ask them questions that they cannot merely answer with a yes or no. Start your questions with the journalist's five Ws and an H—who, what, when, where, why, and how. To that list, you can add open-ended questions that ask them to "describe" or that start with "How many of you think, feel, or believe . . ." This last question gives those answering some comfort that there may be other people who feel the way they do and makes them believe they won't be the only one raising their hand in answer to your question.

Let Them Talk While You Listen

The voir dire process is a terrifying one for most lawyers, who are typically control freaks. It's not like direct or cross-examination, where you know what the witnesses will say and can thoroughly prepare to deal with those limited areas. In jury selection, no matter how much you prepare, you have no idea what may come out of the mouths of some of these prospective jurors. Jury selection is like walking across a tightrope without a net.

Many lawyers cope with their fear of jury selection—the time in trial they are most out of control—by doing all the talking. The more you talk, the less you learn. Ask your question, then be quiet and listen to the answers. Do not explain things to them. Let them explain things to you. That is the best way to gather the most information possible.

---

2. A copy of this document, called "Supplemental Jury Questionnaire," is available at http://www.trialguides.com/resources/downloads/changing-laws.

Start a Polarized Debate

The most honest information comes out in jury selection when the jurors pick sides on the issues that are important to your case. When one juror stakes out an extreme position on an issue, it allows you to find all those who feel the same way, either directly or through body language, nodding in support, or reacting negatively.

For example, in a police shooting case, you might ask, "How many of you believe that when a police officer shoots someone, that person must have done something wrong?" Then ask follow-up questions to find out: "Why do you believe that?" Then look for others who believe the same: "How many of you believe the same thing?" After finding all those people, you would ask, "How many of you feel differently, and believe that sometimes police officers shoot people without good cause or without that person having done anything wrong?"

My friend Don Keenan advocates a direct approach in setting up the polarizing questions. He sets out both sides of the debate up front with polarized statements like this: "There are some people who believe there are police officers who sometimes shoot people for no reason, without that person having done anything wrong. On the other hand, there are those who believe when a police officer shoots someone, that person must have done something wrong. Which way do you lean?"[3]

Other lawyers, like Tom Rhodes, just set out the defense side of the polarizing statement. For example, "When a police officer shoots someone, they must have deserved it." He then puts up a chart that may look something like this:

STRONGLY AGREE	AGREE	DISAGREE	STRONGLY DISAGREE
1	2	3	4

3. This technique just scratches the surface of Don's knowledge on jury selection. To learn fully about this technique, read his book, *Reptile* (New York: Balloon Books, 2009), or, better yet, take one of his nationwide seminars for plaintiffs' lawyers only.

He asks every juror to respond with a numerical score to every statement he makes, then he adds up their numerical scores to determine which jurors are best for his case.

Finally, you can use current events in the news to start the debate on a topic. When you are asking about something that is one step removed from the jurors, they sometimes reveal their true feelings more readily. In the police shooting case, you might ask them about their views on the Rodney King beating or, if you lived in my hometown of Albuquerque, you might ask them about the shooting death of a homeless man named James Boyd, who was killed as the police tried to arrest him for illegally camping in the foothills. The video of that shooting was posted on YouTube and sparked a series of protests.

Don't Be Judgmental

Nothing will stop the flow of information like a judging "tsk, tsk," even if it is under your breath. Even worse is asking that the juror be excused for cause in front of the other panel members. No one else will talk to you about their true feelings and risk public humiliation. No matter how abhorrent the opinion being given, thank the prospective juror for his or her honest response. You should mean it. If the candidate had not been honest with you, you would not know that you needed to strike him or her.

No Note Taking

How would you feel if someone you were having a conversation with at a cocktail party began writing down everything that you said? Chances are you would stop talking to the person who was writing down your comments. The prospective jurors feel the same way. Nothing stops the flow of information like you stopping to write down what they are saying to you.

No matter how small your office, you cannot afford to do voir dire alone and try to keep track of the information being provided by the jurors. If you do not have the resources to hire a jury consultant, then have a friend, a secretary, an associate, or some intuitive person from off the street be responsible for writing down the information provided by the jurors. This will free you to maintain eye contact with each potential juror and carry on a conversation that encourages them to provide more information.

REMIND THE JURY ABOUT TRUTHS THEY ALREADY KNOW

Even if you had weeks for voir dire rather than the half day we are usually granted, you would not be able to educate jurors out of their strongly held beliefs and biases that they have built up from a lifetime of their own experiences. You can discover and discuss their belief systems by reminding them of some of the basic truths they already know, that may be important in your case.

No Lecturing, Make Them Think

How much information do you remember from all of those classroom lectures you heard in high school or college? Unless the speaker was unusually dynamic, you probably don't remember much. Most learning comes not from someone telling you what to think but from thinking things out yourself. The same is true for your prospective jurors.

You will get nowhere by telling them what to think. Avoid the standard lawyer questions you hear in voir dire that begin with the following:

♦ I'm sure we can all agree that _____.

♦ Do you all agree that you will judge this case by the preponderance of the evidence standard, that is, "more likely true than not true"?

♦ By your silence, I assume all of you can be fair and impartial to my client.

None of these lecturing-type statements get you anywhere with the jury. Jurors are unlikely to challenge you on a statement of a legal principle, even if they disagree, and certainly will not admit they don't have the faintest idea what you are talking about. Some will nod their heads, most will do nothing, and you will have no idea about their true feelings.

Instead, you can explore their belief system by reminding them about some of the unique challenges they may be facing as jurors in your case. Do you remember the Socratic method? That is how we learned to think like lawyers and how the jurors can learn to do their jobs. Remember, many of the things they will be asked to do are new to them. They may never have thought about how they will accomplish these tasks. Asking them questions about how they will judge credibility will tell you much about their thinking process and will educate both you and them along the way. Consider the following questions:

- How many of you have ever had to decide between two people (your kids, your employees) who was telling the truth?

- How did you go about determining who was telling the truth between those two people?

- What factors were important to you in making that determination?

- Can you think of some reasons why a person (or your children) might lie? (You might go to several jurors for the answers to these questions. They will probably come up with the reasons pertinent to your case—for money, to get out of trouble, for revenge. If not, then ask whether they have ever seen people lie for those reasons.)

- Are there some things you shouldn't use in deciding whether one person is telling the truth and another is not?

  » How about the race of the person? Why shouldn't that be used?

» How about a person's occupation? Why shouldn't that be used?

» How about the sex of the person? Why shouldn't that be used?

Intersperse Questions with Facts

In Texas you can give your opening statement in voir dire. In Arizona, you can give a brief opening before jury selection begins. For those of you who practice in those jurisdictions, have at it. Everywhere else, you have to intersperse your questions with facts.

Although most judges feel voir dire is not a time to give your complete opening statement, you have to give the jury some idea of what your case is about in order for them to intelligently evaluate their own biases and give you honest answers to your questions. Once prospective jurors have an understanding of the facts of the case, they are more easily able to identify and tell you about their own personal biases.

In truth, lawyers don't eliminate jurors as much as jurors eliminate themselves by an honest recitation of their potential prejudices. That works best the more facts they know about the case. Even the most restrictive judges should understand that the jury has to know something about the case to (a) respond to your questions and (b) not get angry that you are asking these personal questions for no reason. For example, it would be rude to ask for a show of hands of all those women who have been raped or had family members raped, without first explaining that your case involves a sexual assault.

Can They Walk in Your Client's Shoes?

One of the biggest mistakes lawyers make in jury selection is to assume that if a juror has an experience just like their client, say a severe back injury, that juror will be sympathetic toward the client. This is not necessarily true. In fact, people who have suffered severe back injuries may be the jurors who lead the charge against awarding money to your client because no one gave them money for the pain they have lived with all their lives.

In order to evaluate how they will react to your case, you need to ask them how their own experience affected them. What did they do after they were injured? Did they ever consider filing a lawsuit, or are they someone who would never consider such a thing?

You can best understand a person's position by being asked to argue for it. If jurors state negative opinions toward your client's case, test the strength of their convictions, or bias in the case, by asking them how they would go about convincing someone else of the position they have just rejected. Those who are unable to do so may be so thoroughly entrenched that you wish to seek a cause challenge. Those who are able to see the other side may make good jurors.

ESTABLISH RAPPORT

The best way to establish a rapport with a jury is to be honest with them. That means being honest about some of your concerns, your own fears about their views, and your views about the judicial system.

Most importantly, you must ask the things that scare you the most. Each case has its own unique challenges and problems. There is no way to give an exhaustive list of the scary issues in a plaintiff's case. Following are some of the things that should scare you the most in a civil case:

- Your client's psychiatric or mental health history.

- Your client's past criminal history.

- Your client's poor memory.

- Your client's status as an undocumented worker or, as the defense will call him or her, an illegal alien.

♦ Your client's inability to speak English or speaking English with an accent.

♦ Your client's failure to file tax returns, a crime that makes it difficult for you to claim lost wages.

♦ Your client's abuse of alcohol or drugs.

♦ Your client's invisible injuries such as soft tissue, post traumatic stress disorder (PTSD), or mild traumatic brain injury.

♦ Your client's age—either a very young child or a nursing home resident, both ends of life's spectrum make it difficult for jurors to quantify the value of life.

♦ Your client's poor health or physical disabilities before his or her injury or death.

♦ The jury's fear of closing their own local hospital or driving doctors out of town if they find against them in a medical malpractice case.

♦ The jury's fear of driving up their own insurance rates or taxes (in a case against a municipality) with a large damages award.

♦ The jury's expectations about personal responsibility.

♦ The jury's perception of frivolous lawsuits, runaway juries, and "jackpot justice."

♦ The jury's opinions about low-impact auto collisions.

♦ The jury's perception of infallibility of, or favored status for, police officers, doctors, or other professions.

As we prepared to select the jury that would hear Elizabeth Garcia's case, there were several attitudes that scared us. Rather than bury those issues, we asked about all of them to determine which jurors could set them aside and which jurors could not.

24

Jury and Trial Highlights in Elizabeth's Case

The jury we picked was a remarkable collection of people with lots of life experience. There were five men and seven women, ranging in age from thirty-two to ninety-three, all with at least a high school diploma and most with some college. There were four retirees, a realtor, a winemaker, a mechanical engineer, an electrical contractor, a graphic designer, the owner of a paint company, and two retired teachers—the job Elizabeth Garcia had hoped to have some day.

The names of the people we hoped would become the heroes in the case were Jean Lehman, forewoman; Thomas Cliff; Darrah Nagle; Riette Mugleston; Elaine Lucero; Larry Trout; Wallace Borkenhagen; Mark Jacobs; Angela Pacheco; Carol Johnson; John Delaney; and Brenda Quintana.[1]

The questions we asked in voir dire were about their own experiences with, and knowledge of, convenience stores and convenience store crime. Were any of them ever afraid for themselves,

---

1. The jury in this case was extremely proud of their work, and we were honored to work with them. I am still in touch with forewoman Jean Lehman.

their children, or grandchildren when going into a convenience store late at night? If they had worked in a convenience store themselves, how did they feel about the experience? We also asked them about their views on an employer's obligation to make a workplace safe and whether any of them had ever asked for safety changes.

The thing that scared us the most in this case were people who might believe that there is nothing a business owner can do to prevent or reduce crime, that crime was inevitable. Remember that the jury might get to compare the criminal's intentional acts with the Allsup's corporation's negligence. Our concern was that a person who believed in the inevitability of crime would likely place all of the blame on the killer, Paul Lovett. With those few people stricken from the jury, we hoped we had a group of people who would recognize the dangerous conditions Allsup's had created for its customers and minimum-wage workers on the graveyard shift and be courageous enough to do something about it.

TRIAL HIGHLIGHTS

Backed with an incredible PowerPoint slideshow in opening statement (prepared by my law partner Allegra Carpenter), I told the jury the case was about the Allsup's corporation's broken promises, broken rules, and broken alarm system.

I went on to tell them the story about the broken promises to the families of those killed. Everyone I've told you about came in to testify before the jury. Eva Pellissier rasped out her story, the scar on her throat visible above her collar. Robert Christiansen came to talk about his murdered sister. The cross section of different Americans who had worked for the company told stories of the assaults and batteries they suffered and the terror they had experienced every night they went to work in an Allsup's store.

Hobbs Police Chief Tony Knott testified about his conversation with Mark Allsup and his warning a year before Elizabeth Garcia took her job that if Allsup's did not upgrade the security in its stores, someone would be murdered. We played the prison testimony of convenience store robber Brian Nash for the jury via videotape.

Our expert witness, former Gainesville Police Chief Wayland Clifton, was particularly effective. After explaining how the ordinance he helped pass in Gainesville, which required two clerks on the graveyard shift, eliminated all murders and rapes and made a dramatic difference in all other types of crime, we asked him to do something a little different.

We asked him, how would he deliberately design a convenience store that would attract criminals? His answer follows:

> First, you would remove all the high-intensity lighting on the perimeter of the property to create a "fishbowl" effect, where prospective criminals could hide in the parking lot and wait, unseen, in the dark until the clerk was alone. Next, you would make sure there were no security cameras in the store so criminals would have no fear of being caught. Then you would remove the second clerk and put just one clerk, preferably a woman, who would be seen as more vulnerable, alone in the store. Of course, you would dim the lights around the entrance of the store and perhaps put a lot of posters in the windows, so the clerk couldn't see out and passing police cars couldn't see in. Finally, you would stock the store with items that criminals could not get anywhere else after the bars closed at 2:00 a.m., things like cigarettes, beer, and hard liquor.[2]

As demonstrated with a powerful PowerPoint slide, one by one, we visually removed all the standard safety devices discussed by Chief Clifton to create a dangerous store. Once all of those devices were removed and the store staffed by a lone woman

---

2. *McConnell v. Allsup's*, Wayland Clifton testimony.

clerk, what remained was an Allsup's convenience store—a place designed to attract criminals.[3]

The true anchor for our damages, to help the jury determine the value of Elizabeth Garcia's life, came not from our wonderful economist, Brian McDonald—who gave a range of $5 million to $6 million for the statistical value of an average person's life—but from the person Allsup's called to defend its own conduct: Barbara Allsup.

Mrs. Allsup was raised in a small Texas town, where, after completing her high school education, she became a bookkeeper in the convenience store business that she and her husband, Lonnie, started. On cross-examination, I asked her about her experience:

Q: Your company, Allsup's Convenience Stores, Inc., over the years, has regularly made or had $300 million in sales over the last several years, has it not, ma'am?

A: No. I think that's not—that's a figure that we achieved, but it hasn't been that way for several years.

Q: Okay. You, yourself, only had a high school education; is that right, ma'am?

A: That is correct.

Q: And no college?

A: Some college.

Q: With just a high school education and a little bit of college, you helped build the thirty-fifth largest convenience store chain in the nation?

A: Right.

Q: You are always in the top fifty, aren't you, Ms. Allsup?

A: I think so.

---

3. A copy of this PowerPoint, called "PowerPoint Allsup's Stores," is available at http://www.trialguides.com/resources/downloads/changing-laws.

Q: You, meaning Allsup's Convenience Stores, are one of the most profitable privately-owned companies in the state of New Mexico?

A: I do not know.

Q: You hadn't accomplished that, all that, by the time you were twenty-six years old, had you, ma'am?

A: No.

Q: At twenty-six, you were really just starting out, weren't you?

A: That's—no, earlier than that, yes.

Q: And you taught yourself how to do books and computers?

A: Yes.

Q: And nobody would have predicted at the age of twenty-six that you would have built a convenience store empire in your lifetime; is that right?

A: That's possibly correct . . .

Q: You're not saying in this courtroom that your life is worth more than the life of Elizabeth Garcia, are you?

A: Did I say that?

Q: That's what I'm asking you. You're not saying that, are you, ma'am?

A: Nobody asked me that.

Q: Her life should be worth as much as your life; isn't that right, Ms. Allsup?

A: Well, of course.[4]

The evidence from Barbara Allsup's own lips now justified the jury valuing the life of Elizabeth Garcia, a minimum-wage

---

4. Partial Transcript of Proceedings, *McConnell v. Allsup's*, April 2, 2008 TR-24-25 & 31.

worker who wanted to become a teacher, to be the same as the value of the life of Barbara Allsup, a multi-million-dollar-a-year business owner. This admission on cross-examination allowed us to argue in closing that if one twenty-six-year-old woman like Barbara Allsup could achieve such massive financial success over her lifetime, couldn't a smart, hardworking woman like Elizabeth Garcia do the same? All the jury had to do was figure out the amount of money Mrs. Allsup made.

Although it was difficult for our punitive damages economist Dwight Grant to determine from the sparse financial documents that the Allsup's corporation produced, it appeared that from just the convenience store company alone Lonnie and Barbara Allsup split approximately $15 million in profits (5 percent profit on $300 million in sales) in good years. The net value of just the Allsup's convenience store corporation was between $120 million and $500 million. Our economist said that with those financials, the amount of money for punitive damages necessary to make an impression without bankrupting the corporation was between $60 million and $70 million.

At that point in the trial, we thought the evidence and damages were coming in extremely well. Then on Friday, the end of the first week, something unusual happened.

25

Learning to Lose and Taking Care of Your Client

When I was in law school, there were about a dozen women who, like me, wanted to be trial lawyers. Bright-eyed and excited about life's possibilities, we huddled around the carrels in the library, trying to figure out the best pathway to becoming the next female Perry Mason. It has always troubled me that of that group of smart, driven women, I am the only one today who is still venturing into the courtroom. Many of my law school girl-friends are no longer even practicing law. What happened?

They made other choices that brought them different kinds of success. Some joined and worked their way up to top management in large companies or government agencies. Some took time away from their profession to raise their children. Some found satisfaction working for nonprofit organizations. Many of them tried the courtroom but quit after the first time they lost a case. Why would losing a case have such a life-changing effect for my generation of women?

The Classroom vs. Sports

Because we were not allowed to play sports, my generation of women never learned how to lose. The one place we were allowed to compete was in the classroom, where our success depended on our own efforts. If we worked hard enough, we got an A and made it to the top of the class. If we didn't work hard enough, we failed.

The classroom does not teach the lessons you learn on the field or court when playing sports. In sports, no matter how hard you work, no matter how good you are, on any given day or in any given game, your opponent can beat you. Sometimes you lose when your opponent is playing way above his or her abilities, or because of a ball's errant bounce, or because a referee didn't see the foul. None of those things are your fault.

Although you never come to like it, losing teaches you that control is an illusion. You can work hard to tilt the odds in your favor, but you can never predict the outcome of a contest. As a result of all the things that are beyond your control, you can't take losing personally.

The other lesson you learn from losing is that, no matter how painful the loss, after you crawl into bed and pull the covers over your head, the sun still comes up the next morning. There is a bitter taste in your mouth that sometimes lasts for months while you replay over and over all the things you could have done differently. The sun comes up again. The ache subsides. You survive. You learn from your mistakes. So long as you don't quit, you are better the next time, even though that is no guarantee of winning.

Unlike many of my girlfriends who only competed in the classroom, I was fortunate to have parents who encouraged me to play tennis, even though their reasons for doing so were a little suspect. My mother thought learning to play tennis would be a good way to meet boys. She didn't expect me to take it quite so seriously or competitively. The first time I came home after trouncing the boy I had been dating, my mother was horrified.

"You aren't supposed to beat them," she told me, with an appalled look on her face. "Not if you want them to ask you out again." It was too late. I liked beating the boys. Sometimes they beat me back. I learned to lose and to understand that my own self-worth wasn't tied up with the loss.

In 1972, the year before I graduated from high school, the United States Congress passed, and President Richard Nixon signed into law, Title IX, the federal legislation that would encourage public schools and colleges to fund women's sports. Although forty-two years later there is still not equal funding for men's and women's sports, we have come a long way. Girls are playing soccer, basketball, volleyball, and other sports from grade school to college. They are learning to lose—and to win. I'm hoping those skills will encourage more women to come into the courtroom to fight, not for a championship ring, but as warriors for justice.

LEARNING HOW TO LOSE

Being a trial lawyer takes courage. If your cause is righteous, losing a case in the courtroom is much worse than losing at sports. If you have never lost a case, you are not trying enough of the close-call cases, those that you can't settle and so you must try. Unlike the website description provided by Mr. Y. Kevin Williams, I admit that I have lost some jury trials—five of the more than 130 cases I have taken to trial.

As is human nature, I remember my failures in greater detail than my victories. One loss was because the jury couldn't get past my client's Middle Eastern heritage and our horrible expert witness; one was because opposing counsel was allowed to circumvent the court's rulings and cheat; three were close factual calls that could have gone either way. Because of those losses and the glaring knowledge from sports that I can lose any case, no matter how well it's going, I have to be honest with my clients about that possibility.

What Does Justice Look Like for the Client?

Lawyers get so wrapped up sometimes in issues of proof and persuasion that they forget whose case it really is. When a client or their family has been wronged, the ultimate decision about settlement is theirs, not mine. When children are involved, no matter how much glory (or higher fee) you may achieve through a huge verdict, all of your decisions must be driven by what is best for the children. Among other things, this means appointing a guardian *ad litem* to make sure any settlement money is preserved and protected solely for the benefit of the children. One of the biggest considerations where there are children involved is the excruciatingly long time it takes for a case to work its way through the legal system and the warp speed at which children grow up.

It took six years for Elizabeth Garcia's case to get to trial. Add three to four years on top of that for appeal. A healthy adult can wait six to ten years for justice. A child, with immediate needs for housing, clothing, and schooling, cannot. The defendants you sue know that.

How do you address your clients' needs without letting the defendants take advantage of those needs?

You try to figure out how much money it will take to make a real difference in their lives. For one woman, whose husband had been a day laborer all his life before he was crushed to death by a long-broken runaway tractor his employer required him to jump-start with a screwdriver, all she wanted was $10,000 to fix the roof on the modest house she had lived in all her life. We helped her understand his life was worth more than that, but it was the ability to buy a new roof that made her life better.

Families Donating to Causes

Other people have used settlement money to make a difference by donating to worthy causes in the name of their loved ones. In one of my cases, a hospital technician did not alert anyone to the fact that an EKG showed a local prosecutor, Wayne Jordon, was having a heart attack. He dropped dead in the courtroom five days later. His widow, Sandra Grisham, donated settlement money from the wrongful death lawsuit against the hospital to train other assistant district attorneys in the job her husband loved so much. As of this writing, the National District Attorneys Association is in the process of naming one of its courtrooms the Wayne Jordon Memorial Courtroom.

Wayne Jordon

Twenty-nine-year-old Nina Nilssen was murdered after a cruise line dropped her off on a dangerous beach in Antigua where others had been attacked. Her parents Morten and Katherine used the settlement money to set up a foundation in their daughter's name to provide scholarships in art education at ninasfund.org.

Nina Nilssen

Eighteen-year-old Manoa Jojola, an actor and musician, was struck and killed by a driver fleeing police in a high-speed chase through the heart of Albuquerque. His parents, Ted Jojola and Dely Alcantara, requested and obtained police department policy changes, then donated the settlement money to the Tricklock Theater Company in their son's name.

Manoa Jojola

If there are surviving children who need to be raised and taken care of, how much money do they need to replace what they have lost, understanding that you can never replace their mother? On the other hand, faced with a corporation or business that refuses to acknowledge and change the dangerous conditions in its workplace or product, how do you come up with a number for damages that will force it to change?

TARGET NUMBERS AND CHANGES

Our approach to settling a case is not the traditional one of picking a target number, starting high and then negotiating lower and lower, down to your target number as the case proceeds. As discussed in the chapter on transformative law, if a defendant agrees to make safety changes early in the case, we will settle the case for a lower amount. Once that opportunity has passed, either with or without mediation, we often file an Offer of Settlement for the bottom dollar amount we will take.[1]

Once that formal offer expires, unlike traditional negotiations, our settlement numbers go up rather than down, barring some dramatic turn in the case. As discovery proceeds and we gather more and more information, our case usually gets better rather than worse. If the trial goes well, those settlement numbers increase. After Allsup's and its insurance company rejected our early request to change their practices and settle for $3 million, we finished our investigation and defeated their motions for summary judgment.

In December of 2007, the year before trial, we made an Offer of Settlement in the amount of $17 million. Although that amount could not replace the loss of their mother, it was enough money, even after our one-third attorney fee and the huge costs in the case, to be put away in a trust for each child by our personal representative, Mary Ann McConnell. The money would take care of their needs in a way that would ensure they could go to college, travel, and have a head start on a successful life.

Allup's did not accept our offer within the ten-day period, and so it was automatically withdrawn after ten days—a good thing, because something happened in trial that changed the dynamics of the case and made us realize our offer of settlement had been too low.

---

1. The New Mexico Rules of Civil Procedure, NMRA 1-068, allow plaintiffs as well as defendants to make formal Offers of Settlement that expire after ten days. If a plaintiff does better than the offer at trial, then the other side has to pay double costs from the date of the offer forward.

26

A TURNING POINT IN THE CASE AND CLOSING ARGUMENT

Remember, the Allsup's corporation had two juries in the courtroom: the real one made up of twelve citizens and two alternates that we picked after jury selection, and their own shadow jury that they paid to sit in the back of the courtroom. The problem with using a shadow jury in a small town like Santa Fe (population 60,000) is that it is hard to keep a secret. The bigger the secret, the harder it is to keep.

At the end of the first week of trial, on Friday morning, the lawyers on the other side came in looking terrible, like they had slept in their clothes. When one of the junior lawyers on the team stood up to argue a motion before they brought in the jury, his voice rose higher and higher as he argued, until he was almost in tears. What was going on?

When you are in trial, between working on your direct examinations, organizing the exhibits you will use each day, and preparing your witnesses to testify, it is not unusual to get only a couple hours of sleep each night. I wondered whether the defense team was getting even less sleep than we were since in addition to everything they had to do for the trial, they had to wait until the jury consultant debriefed the shadow jury, analyze the information, and then meet with the consultant at 9:00 or 10:00 p.m. to discuss the shadow jurors' impressions of the case. This meant they couldn't start retooling their case and prepare for the next day until after 10:00 p.m.

We didn't have to wait long to figure out why the defense team seemed so disoriented and distressed. By noon on Friday, word had filtered down to us about a possible source of their discomfort. On Thursday night, just four days into the trial, the shadow jurors not only wanted to rule for the Garcia family, but when asked about how much in damages they were considering, gave the jury consultant a staggering number—$100 million.

This trickle-down rumor came not from any of the shadow jurors, who all honored the confidentiality agreement they signed. Where did the information come from? When given a shocking number like that, the numerous lawyers on the other side presumably went home and talked to their families about the case. Those family members apparently talked to others, and by noon, the secret was out and transmitted to our side.

On Monday, we began getting calls from AIG to discuss settlement. By then, we had another settlement number, which we would stick to throughout the second week of trial. The first calls we received came from AIG's insurance adjuster. Having never made any significant settlement offer before trial, she began low. To every number she came up with, we responded with our same firm amount. After a few days of back and forth, we started getting calls from the senior lawyer from AIG's Atlanta firm, Billy Gunn.

"You know," he patiently explained to me in his Southern accent, "the way settlement negotiations are supposed to go is that we raise our offer, and then you reduce your offer, back and forth, until we agree on an amount."

"Sorry," I said. "Maybe that's how they do it in Atlanta, but that's not how we do it here in New Mexico." Why would we pick a settlement number and continue to negotiate after learning of the shadow jury's view of the case?

For one thing, the rumor we had heard might have been incorrect. Like the childhood game of telephone, where one person whispers something to another around a circle and by the time the story gets to the last person, it has changed, the number that the shadow jury supposedly gave may have been inflated. Even if what we heard was true, the least useful information from a focus group or shadow jury, to try and predict what a real jury will do, is the amount of damages.

Finally, what would happen if the real jury rather than the shadow jury actually awarded $100 million, a verdict twice the amount of any verdict ever awarded in the state of New Mexico? Allsup's would appeal the verdict to the New Mexico Court of Appeals and then to the New Mexico Supreme Court. The enormity of the verdict would increase the chance that it would be reversed on appeal. Even if it was upheld, because the appeal would take another four to five years, Elizabeth Garcia's children would be grown up before they saw a dime of the money.

The phone calls and negotiations continued every day while the trial went into a second week, through the testimony of Barbara Allsup, defense expert witness Merlyn Moore, and a manager, Deb Carr, who still worked for the company and tried to defend its dangerous practices. As the trial continued, AIG kept raising its offer in phone calls during and after trial. In response, we stayed at the same number we had selected with the input of Mary Ann McConnell and Victorina Garcia. Then it was time for closing argument.

Closing argument is the time when a trial lawyer takes her heart out of her chest and lays it on the jury rail. The jury can accept it or crush it. My closing argument in this case was intensely personal. It involved, for the first time in my life, a little singing. Rather than set out the entire hour-long closing verbatim, the following is paraphrased. Passages taken from the closing argument are indented.

> You have heard over the last couple of weeks the tale of two families. The first is the Allsup's Convenience Store family: Lonnie Allsup, Barbara Allsup, and

Mark Allsup, the people who ran that company and made the calculated risk to have a store that attracted crime. Keeping it that way benefited them and actually resulted in money in their pocket by not fixing it. They made the decision because it benefited them not to fix any of their stores.

And then you have the Garcia family, which is a family of teachers. The Allsups didn't see Elizabeth that way. They saw her only as a minimum-wage clerk. You on the jury know better than that. You know they are a family of teachers and they are the ones who bore all of the risk in this case and suffered the worst loss you could ever suffer.

Then, because I believed that we had already proved liability, I did something I had never done before. I started the argument with damages, in this case, the loss of the most important person in anyone's life—their mother.

The greatest fear of every child . . . is the fear of losing your mother, the fear that you will be abandoned. It is the fear that makes us weep on the first day of school when she drops us off because we think she's not coming back. It is the fear that causes us to not want to go to sleep at night because we are concerned that she might not be there in the morning when we wake up. It is that fear and the importance of a mother in your life that makes grown men, when they are dying on the battlefield, call out not for their girlfriends, not for their lovers, but for their mothers, as they are dying. A mother is the most important thing in our life. It is the source of where everything else comes from. Until we learn her unconditional love, we really aren't fit to go into the world, and, once we learn it, we take her with us wherever we go.

It is to assuage this fear that the children's book *The Runaway Bunny*[1] was written. The whole point of that book is a promise to your child that no matter what, no matter how naughty you are, I won't abandon you. I will come for you. I will be there for you. I will be there for you every day of your life.

I learned about the depth of loss caused by the death of a mother from my grandmother Edith McGinn. Her mother died from tuberculosis when Edith was about five years old, a little younger than Xavier. Her last memory of her mother was hugging her through the bars of the gate in the sanitarium where she was unsuccessfully treated for her illness.

When I was a kid, my Irish Catholic grandmother would take me to Mass and we would kneel down and she would always light a candle every Sunday. And I would say to my grandmother, "What are you lighting these candles for?" And she would say, "I am praying to God that I will always be here for my children."

And that seemed kind of bizarre to me at the time, because her "child" was my parent who was a grown person, and why would you still want to be here for your grown child? Yet that was her prayer every Sunday for the rest of her life . . . because of what she herself had been through, because the worst thing in her life was that she had lost her mother . . . at a young age.

One of the songs that my grandmother McGinn loved the most was the love song, "If Ever I Would Leave You" from the stage play and movie musical *Camelot*. I sang a few lines for the jury to remind them of the tune:

1. Margaret Wise Brown, illustrated by Clement Hurd, *The Runaway Bunny* (New York: Harpers, 1942).

If ever I would leave you, it wouldn't be in summer,
seeing you in summer, I never could go.

The same was true for springtime, autumn, and winter, ending
with:

Oh no, not in springtime, summer, winters, or fall.
No, never could I leave you at all.

    Whenever I hear that song, I don't think of
Guinevere and Lancelot and their problems. I
think of my grandmother. And it made me think
in this case, if you could pick—if you could pick
a time and it was your choice to leave your child,
when would it be?

    When I was twenty-six years old, my daughter
was one and I was a single mother like Elizabeth
Garcia. And I think maybe, if you had to pick a
time, maybe at one year old would be the best
time to leave your child, because they don't know
you then, really. They don't really have a memory
of you. Maybe that would be the best and then
somebody else could come along and they could
raise them and they would never know.

    And then you think, well, maybe not, because
then they'd always wonder what you were like. So
how about at age five? How about leaving them
at five? Could you do that then? Right at the time
when they're about to start school and they really
need you and they really need somebody to take
them the first time and explain what's going to
happen. It would be almost impossible leaving
them at five . . . Jerome's age.

    Or maybe six. Then I think about all the time I
would sit in bed with my daughter and read books
to her at that age. That's about the age where you
get to cuddle up next to them. I never know if it's us

comforting them or them comforting us, because it's such a wonderful experience where they've had their bath and smell so wonderful. So maybe at seven, Xavier's age back then. . . . That would be a tough age to leave your child, too, once they really know you and understand what you're like, to then vanish into nothing. That would be really hard.

My daughter is now twenty-seven, and I think, well, maybe I could leave her now. But then who would answer her phone calls in the middle of the night? What should I do about this job? Should I take this class? It would be so hard to leave her now.

Think of all the things I would have missed if I had left her earlier . . . although [Elizabeth's children] have missed so much in the last six years of their mom, there's so much more [that will happen in the future]. Elizabeth won't be here to pick out Cene's wedding dress for her. She won't be here to help her children with college essays . . . there's so much that happens in the future that they will miss with their mother.

So the point is, there is never a good time to leave your child. Never, never, never. But the worst time, it seems to me, is once you've already known what it is to be loved by someone like that, and then, have them taken away.

So let's talk about what you've seen in this case about the effects on these children of that very loss. They lost their mom two weeks after their last Christmas together. Cene has the most magical way of dealing with this, you've heard from her grandmother. She just denies that it's happened and believes that her mom is everywhere she goes; that she sees her in the audience of her ballet performance; that she tells her grandmother that she's there, I know she's watching me, and it is a marvelous coping measure. But you know and Cene knows that she's not there, as evidenced by the time they found Cene in the bathroom by herself at a Christmas party, when everybody else's parents were there, crying and crying and crying because she was the only one there without a mom. So she can pretend that her mom is there, and it may be easier for Cene, because every time she looks in the mirror, her mom's face is looking back at her. She looks just like her mom. So in that respect, she's carrying her with her.

And then, there is Jerome, who is dealing with it in the most interesting way; that is, to tell me all these stories about [his] mom so he can pretend like he remembers it. "Oh, yeah, we used to eat whole-wheat pancakes, I remember." He's trying to manufacture memories because he doesn't have many of his own. So he is dealing with it in his own way, too, and coping in his own way.

Of course, the person who is having the most difficulty is Xavier. If they could go back and not have him in that room when the . . . police officer arrived . . . but nobody knew he was standing there when that happened. And he knew, instantly, because he was almost eight, that his mom was not coming back and went out into the yard and screamed. And he's been screaming inside ever since.[2]

I then asked the jury to award an amount for each child's relationship with their mother so that when they were grown and told the amount of the award, they would know how much the jury valued the loss of a mother, their mother, Elizabeth Garcia. I talked about how the decisions made by the Allsups had endangered not just Elizabeth, but all different kinds of people:

2. Partial Transcript of Proceedings, *McConnell v. Allsup's*, April 7, 2008.

[M]others, fathers, young people, old people, all different races, Hispanic, African American, white, everybody, all kinds of people working in these stores. Not just all kinds of people working in these stores but all kinds of people coming into these stores, across all classes. All of us are going into the stores. Our kids are stopping by at night to get gas or pick up some candy bars.[3]

I told the jury that important cases like this were the reason I loved being a lawyer.

Because not all lawsuits are frivolous. . . . There are necessary lawsuits like this that embody the greatest part of what our American judicial system is. Because, you know, in most countries, somebody who is a minimum-wage worker . . . never has a chance to ever come to court and try to hold the mighty and powerful accountable. This is one of the few countries in the world where that could happen. In other places, your power, your influence, your money prevents [justice] from ever taking place. You never even get here. And only in America could somebody like Elizabeth Garcia and her family think that they could come here and then have people who can't be influenced, twelve people on the jury, decide what's right and what's wrong in this case.

In this regard, you have more power than any of us here. I can't make Allsup's do what's right. The Judge can't make Allsup's do what's right. Only you can. They have had every chance in the world to do so, and they have said, "How dare you tell me that I have to change." But they can't say that to you,

3. *McConnell v. Allsup's*, closing argument by Randi McGinn.

because what you decide will make a change in this particular case.[4]

When we got to the issue of punitive damages, we asked the jury to divest the company of the money it pocketed by breaking its promises to its employees and their families and its decision not to implement an industry-standard second clerk. The jury could choose between the twenty-seven years since Lonnie Allsup promised Amanda Rockford's mother and little brother, Robert Christiansen, that they would never make a woman work alone again, or the sixteen years since the industry learned from the Gainesville study how a second clerk would reduce crime.

Although Allsup's saved over $6 million a year as a result of its decision across all 300 plus of its stores, Judge Ortiz limited our request to the 116 New Mexico stores.

Using the $2.2 million Allsup's saved every year in its 116 New Mexico stores, we created an animated slide for closing that added it all up. Using twenty-seven years, Allsup's had made $59.4 million by its decisions and had made $35.2 million in the sixteen years since the Gainesville study.

We used the shadow jury's rumored $100 million number in a counterintuitive way. When talking about punitive damages, I told the jury some of them might be so mad they wanted to award enough money to put the company out of business or to award an even larger amount, say $300 million (there was a sudden squirming at the defense table), the amount of their gross sales for a year. I asked them not to do so, because

> One, if you award $300 million, you will put out of work the 2,500 minimum-wage clerks who need the jobs. And you've heard it's a lousy job, but people need them in this state to feed their families. And I don't care about the Allsups, but I care about them. And so you can't award an amount of money that will put them out of business.

4. *McConnell v. Allsup's*, closing argument by Randi McGinn.

Secondly, people will say you acted out of passion as opposed to reason . . . which is why we asked an expert to come in and look at their finances and their books and say, what can we award? What is a fair amount to award that won't put them out of business that will be tied to their bad conduct?

You know, there are very few times in your life when you get to make a difference, a real difference that matters not just for you, but for your whole community and even outside New Mexico. And this is one of them. . . . We are hopeful that with your verdict, you will send a message not just to the Allsups, but to any [other] convenience store chains who still think it's okay to calculate the risk and keep the money while you have your minimum-wage clerks face the risk alone at night.

In rebuttal argument, I asked the jury to imagine the two possible futures that would occur because of their decision. If they ruled in favor of Allsup's or awarded a low amount, say just one year of the $2.2 million Allsup's profited by not adding a second clerk, the defense counsel would make an immediate phone call to Lonnie Allsup, who never appeared in the courtroom.

Y. Kevin Williams would call him back at the corporate headquarters in Clovis or perhaps at one of his ranches and say,

"Mr. Allsup, I've got some good news and some bad news. . . . The bad news is you lost the case. The good news is that the jury didn't award $59.4 million, the money you saved over the last twenty-seven years by not putting a second clerk on duty. They only gave $10 million in punitive damages. So, you see, it was a good economic business decision for you to make, because you've saved $49.4 million. So you keep doing what you're doing and saving that money [by not paying for security], because at some point somebody may try to hold you accountable, but you will not be held fully accountable [here]."

Or you can imagine the other statement you can make, which is that a year from now, sometime late at night, you'll be driving somewhere and need gas, and you'll find a convenience store that is fully lit with perimeter lighting and cameras, and you can walk into the store safely and buy whatever you need. And when you do it, smile at the two clerks on duty, because they won't know what you've done here today, but you will, and that will be enough.

After closing argument, Judge Ortiz dismissed the two alternates and our jury of twelve went back to deliberate.

27

THE VERDICT AND ITS
AFTERMATH

For some lawyers, the period of time when the jury is out is extremely stressful. They can't eat and they can't sleep. I am exactly the opposite. Once I have given a case everything I have and poured it all out in closing argument, a sense of peace comes over me. It is in the jury's hands, and there is nothing else I can do. Usually, I am exhausted.

This was how it was in Elizabeth's case. After closing argument, we walked back to our Santa Fe office, a small renovated house near the old courthouse. Even though it was still daylight, I told my law partners that I was going to sleep for the next couple of hours. If the defense lawyers or AIG called wanting to settle, they were to be told I was taking a nap and had asked not to be disturbed.

There were a couple of calls while I was sleeping and a great deal of frustration when my partners refused to wake me up to talk to the other side. The longer the jury stayed out, the closer and closer the other side came to our settlement number. By that time, Allsup's had its private attorney pushing the insurance company to settle the case to avoid the bad publicity they expected from a large verdict.

Should we let the verdict be rendered to vindicate Elizabeth and all the other clerks who had been raped, beaten, stabbed, or killed in an Allsup's store? Or should we take care of Elizabeth's children now? What would you do in the same situation? Because of the insurance company's dithering over terms, it turned out we were able to do both.

The ice broke when Allsup's agreed as part of the settlement to stop its efforts to repeal or override the New Mexico EIB regulations for convenience stores. With that concession, AIG came to a number that would resolve the case. As part of the settlement, they required that the amount be kept secret from the public, and so I cannot tell you what the case settled for. Separate from the settlement we reached, six years after Elizabeth Garcia's death, Allsup's wrote a check for $7,714 for the funeral expenses Victorina paid out of her savings, the claim the workers' compensation carrier refused to honor because it claimed Elizabeth was not killed at work.

Because the insurance company took so long working out the details, the jury knocked on the door and told us they had a verdict just as we were putting the settlement on the record with Judge Ortiz. When Judge Ortiz brought the jury in and told them we had settled the case after all their hard work, there was a collective groan from the jury box.

The forewoman, Jean Lehman, had a question: "Even though the case was settled, is there anything that prevents us from telling what our verdict is?"

Much to the delight of the assembled media representatives in the courtroom, Judge Ortiz said, "No, the jury is free to discuss your decision with anyone, including the press."

As was published in all the local papers the next morning, the jury had unanimously voted to award one of the largest verdicts in New Mexico at that time. They awarded a total of $51.2 million—$30 million in punitive damages; $2 million to each of the children for the loss of their mother ($6 million total); and the jury valued the life of Elizabeth Garcia, the minimum-wage worker who hoped to become a teacher, at $15.2 million.

The jury found that Allsup's had acted willfully in causing the store to be unsafe. It found the corporation 60 percent at fault and the killer, Paul Lovett, 40 percent at fault, something that might have reduced what Allsup's owed for compensatory damages to the family but would not have reduced the award of punitive damages.

AFTER THE VERDICT

After a tense, emotional trial where your client's future is resting on the result, a verdict like this brings relief and the immediate result is that you are able to sleep for about fifteen hours straight. After you are rested, you can better appreciate the wonderful things that happen for your clients and the safety changes that happen for the community.

The Garcia Family

Victorina Garcia went back home to Roswell, where she was able to buy a new house for Xavier, Jerome, and Cene—large enough that each of them could have their own private bedroom and no longer need to share a room.

The rest of the settlement money was placed with a trustee to make sure it would be preserved and managed to take care of the children for the rest of their lives.

Xavier graduated from Goddard High School in 2013 and is currently at the University of New Mexico studying mechanical engineering.

Jerome graduated in 2014 and has been admitted to UNM as well, where he will join his brother in the dorm. He wants to study business.

The youngest, Cene, is in high school and a whiz at biology. Upon graduation, she hopes to study and make her career in forensic science, perhaps using her skills to catch people like the man who killed her mother and will remain in prison for the rest of his life.

Xavier, Jerome, and Cene in 2014, and their house with their own rooms

The Jury

After the trial, the jury forewoman called our office and invited our entire team of lawyers to lunch in Santa Fe with the rest of the jurors. It was a wonderful gathering of people who had made a decision to keep our community and future convenience store workers and customers safer. Jury service was a wonderful experience for these remarkable citizens, even for one of the men who had missed a family vacation to serve on this jury.

They asked, but we could not tell them, the amount of the confidential settlement. They had to trust that we had made sure the children would be protected. Several of the jurors have stayed in touch since the trial to keep up on the progress of Elizabeth's kids.

The Defense Lawyer

And what of Y. Kevin Williams, the defense lawyer who appeared from his website to never have lost a case? His firm press release and his website claim he won this case too. The law firm press release described him as riding to the rescue a week before trial in what was described as a hopeless case for Allsup's. Through his great legal skills and the daylong jury deliberations, he claimed to have intimidated our office into settling the case for what turned out to be a "fraction" of the ultimate verdict. As a former math major, I can tell you that almost any number can be made into a fraction.[1]

Not only is that a disingenuous description of the settlement, which we are bound to keep confidential, but Mr. Williams does not disclose that Allsup's sued AIG's subsidiary insurance company for bad faith. The Allsup's suit claims that the insurer failed to promptly settle the case and avoid all the bad publicity against Allsup's that occurred because of the trial. That case is still awaiting trial.

Our Law Firm

All of my law partners, Allegra, Elicia, and Kathy, are still here at McGinn, Carpenter, Montoya and Love, P.A. (MCML). Katie Curry, the young associate who helped gather all the Allsup's police reports, will join us as a partner next year. We have even hired a great male lawyer, Mike Sievers.

People keep calling us when the worst thing in their lives happens and we try to help, not just with money, but by making a difference. We could use some help out here.

As the United States Supreme Court keeps putting its finger on the scale of justice on the side of corporations, the world needs

---

1. This was a quote from Y. Kevin Williams's press release. We wrote them a letter telling them we thought his press release violated the terms of the confidentiality order. A copy of their press release, called "Press Release Y Kevin Williams," is available at http://www.trialguides.com/resources/downloads/changing-laws.

more women (and men) who are willing to step up and fight for the little guys and gals. Come be a woman warrior. It is one of the world's great jobs. If you work hard, perhaps you will not only change the world, but you might get an insurance company to buy you a conference table.

As a symbol and reminder of AIG's arrogant failure to respond to our early $3 million settlement offer, our law firm, MCML, used part of the money we received from our one-third contingency fee to have a large granite conference table designed and built. It will forever be known in our office as the AIG Memorial Conference Table.

The AIG Memorial Conference Table

Sometimes, late at night, I stop by a New Mexico convenience store, whether I need anything or not. There, behind the counter and monitored by a security camera, are always two clerks. I suspect the workers know nothing of the Garcia family's sacrifice and courage in taking this case all the way to trial.

They do not know about all their fellow workers and their families who testified before the Environmental Improvement Board. They don't know about all the lay and expert witnesses who came to trial to make sure the world knew the truth about the dangers of their late-night jobs. They do not know about Santa Fe Judge Raymond Ortiz, who made sure the family's claims reached a jury. They do not know about the twelve citizens who heard all the evidence and rendered a verdict that served as a warning to all convenience stores in the state to protect their workers and customers.

And I don't tell them. I hand them a couple of dollars for a pack of gum or a Diet Coke and ask them their names. When they hand me back my change, I smile.

"You stay safe," I say, and head back into the night.

INDEX

Downloadable Content

This book refers to a number of items that are available for download from the Trial Guides website. These items may be useful in your law practice, and they further illustrate the principles that Randi teaches in this book. To download these files to your computer, smartphone, or tablet, go to the link below:

http://www.trialguides.com/resources/downloads/changing-laws

Affidavit Eva Pellissier

Eva Pellissier's affidavit is mentioned in chapter 8. This affidavit documents how the Allsup's district manager told her that no woman would ever work alone on the night shift again.

Letter to New Mexico EIB

The Letter to the New Mexico Environmental Improvement Board (EIB) is mentioned in chapters 12 and 16. The employees of the Allsup's Store No. 58 in Tucumcari, New Mexico, wrote this letter describing their working conditions and the Allsup's refusal to make their stores safer.

Motion Gregg McCrary

This motion is referenced in chapter 16. This is the motion we filed to exclude McCrary's testimony from our trial on the basis that it was not grounded in science, was unreliable, and would confuse the jury.

Order Judge Ortiz about Gregg McCrary

This order from Judge Ortiz is referenced in chapter 16. This is the order that Judge Ortiz wrote excluding Gregg McCrary's testimony from trial.

PowerPoint Allsup's Stores

This PowerPoint is referenced in chapter 24. This is based on trial testimony from Gainesville Police Chief Wayland Clifton, as he described a hypothetical convenience store that would be designed to attract criminals.

Press Release Y Kevin Williams

This press release is referenced in chapter 27, where Y. Kevin Williams claimed that he won the case, riding to the rescue a week before trial.

Report Allsup's History of Violence

This report is referenced in chapter 8. This ninety-three-page report details violent crime in Allsup's stores from 1975 to 2002. The report specifically doesn't include any nonviolent crimes such as shoplifting.

Supplemental Jury Questionnaire

This document is referenced in chapter 23. A supplemental jury questionnaire can help you gather information about the jury if your time in jury selection is limited.

Video Jason Wachocki

This video is referenced in chapter 3. Jason Wachocki was killed when he was hit by a corrections officer on his way to work at the Bernalillo County Metropolitan Detention Center. Going to the scene helped us realize that all the police vehicles ignored a stop sign, and this surveillance video was the result.

COLOPHON

Editor: Tina Ricks

Copyeditors: Travis Kremer and Alexandra Haehnert

Proofreader: Patricia Esposito

Indexer: Lucie Haskins

Cover Design: Chris Tegethoff

Interior Design: Laura Lind and Erin E. Davis

ABOUT THE AUTHOR

Interesting Stuff

Randi McGinn is the senior partner in a five-woman, two-man law firm in Albuquerque, New Mexico. She is known for her creativity in the courtroom and her use of demonstrative evidence to visualize opening, direct, cross-examination, and closing argument. She has destroyed adverse witnesses by leaving a pretentious Beverly Hills doctor standing in front of the jury covered with sticky notes and clutching a grapefruit to his chest, by grilling a government snitch until he threw up, and by exposing the fact that a world-renowned polygraph expert had been polygraphing his own sperm cells in the dead of night. In a particularly hard-won police shooting case, the local SWAT officers once put her face on their Christmas piñata and took turns whacking it with a big stick.

Randi started her career by giving birth to daughter Heather, now age thirty-four, the day before the three-day bar examination.

Boring Stuff

Randi is the vice president of the Inner Circle of Advocates. She is double-listed in criminal and civil litigation in *Best Lawyers in America*, and is a fellow in the International Academy of Trial Lawyers. She is a former governor of the American Association for Justice, a past president of the New Mexico Trial Lawyers Association, and a former board member of the National Association of Criminal Defense Lawyers. Randi has taught trial practice for the National Institute for Trial Advocacy and the National Criminal Defense College, and has been an adjunct professor for the University of New Mexico.